GETTING INTO TEACHER TRAINING

Sara Miller McCune founded SAGE Publishing in 1965 to support the dissemination of usable knowledge and educate a global community. SAGE publishes more than 1000 journals and over 800 new books each year, spanning a wide range of subject areas. Our growing selection of library products includes archives, data, case studies and video. SAGE remains majority owned by our founder and after her lifetime will become owned by a charitable trust that secures the company's continued independence.

Los Angeles | London | New Delhi | Singapore | Washington DC | Melbourne

3RD EDITION

GETTING INTO TEACHER TRAINING

BRUCE BOND, JIM JOHNSON, MARK PATMORE,
NINA WEISS & GEOFF BARKER

SAGE | LearningMatters

Learning Matters
An imprint of SAGE Publications Ltd
1 Oliver's Yard
55 City Road
London EC1Y 1SP

SAGE Publications Inc.
2455 Teller Road
Thousand Oaks, California 91320

SAGE Publications India Pvt Ltd
B 1/I 1 Mohan Cooperative Industrial Area
Mathura Road
New Delhi 110 044

SAGE Publications Asia-Pacific Pte Ltd
3 Church Street
#10-04 Samsung Hub
Singapore 049483

Editor: Amy Thornton
Development editor: Geoff Barker
Production controller: Chris Marke
Marketing manager: Dilhara Attygalle
Cover design: Wendy Scott
Typeset by: C&M Digitals (P) Ltd, Chennai, India
Printed and bound in the UK

© 2018 Bruce Bond, Jim Johnson, Mark Patmore,
Nina Weiss & Geoff Barker

First published in 2013
Third edition published in 2018

Library of Congress Control Number: 2017954827

British Library Cataloguing in Publication data

A catalogue record for this book is available from the
British Library.

ISBN 978-1-5264-2779-3 (pbk)
ISBN 978-1-5264-2778-6

At SAGE we take sustainability seriously. Most of our products are printed in the UK using FSC papers and boards.
When we print overseas we ensure sustainable papers are used as measured by the Egmont grading system.
We undertake an annual audit to monitor our sustainability.

Contents

Acknowledgements

We would like to thank the following contributors who responded to questions on applications and interviews to ITT, and shared their thoughts and comments, for the final chapter.

Doreen Challen, *Primary PGCE Tutor, Southampton Education School*
Jean Conteh, *Senior Lecturer in Primary Education, University of Leeds*
Richard English, *Programme Director for the Primary PGCE Course, University of Hull*
Suzanne Horton, *Senior Lecturer in Primary Initial Teacher Education, University of Worcester*
Angela Major, *Principal Lecturer in Education, University of Roehampton*
Ceri Roscoe, *Assistant Head of Primary Programmes with particular responsibility for the BA Primary Education, Manchester Metropolitan University*
Debbie Simpson, *Interim PGCE Primary Programme Leader, University of Cumbria*

We would also like to thank Sam Curran, a recent PGCE student, for his comments informing the student piece in Chapter 6.

The numeracy glossary is reproduced courtesy of the TA © Teaching Agency for Schools. Permission to reproduce TA copyright material does not extend to any material which is identified as being the copyright of a third party or any photographs. Authorisation to reproduce such material would need to be obtained from the copyright holders.

The publishers would like to thank the TA for permission to use the audio icon. This has been taken from the practice Literacy Skills Test on the TA website **www.education.gov.uk** and is the copyright of the Teaching Agency.

About the authors and contributor

Authors

Jim Johnson is an Honorary Fellow of Nottingham Trent University where, until his retirement, he led the English team in the Department of Education.

Bruce Bond has been authoring, editing and reviewing the computerised QTS Literacy Skills Tests since their introduction in 2001/2. Bruce also worked on the development and evaluation of the FE Initial Teacher Training Pilot. He has taught English in the primary, secondary and further education sectors for over 35 years.

Mark Patmore is a former senior lecturer in mathematical education at the School of Education at Nottingham Trent University and is currently an associate lecturer at the University of Derby. He has worked in teacher education with Bishop Grosseste University and with training providers and also provided CPD for teachers of mathematics. After some years as a numeracy consultant for the Teacher Training Agency, Mark was one of the writers for the numeracy skills tests and then became a member of the Test Review Group managed by Alpha*Plus* Consultancy which monitored the writing of the tests.

Mark was chief examiner for the Cambridge Award in Mathematics, and was chief examiner for functional skills in mathematics and has been involved with assessing and verifying a range of educational qualifications. He is the author or co-author of a number of publications for both GCSE and Key Stage 3 Mathematics.

Nina Weiss is currently a Deputy Director at City and Islington Sixth Form College and has worked in the secondary, sixth-form college, FE and HE sectors for almost 40 years as a teacher of English, teacher educator and consultant. Her extensive teacher training experience includes external examining for ITT courses at the UCL Institute of Education, University of Greenwich and University of West London, as well as course leadership of the Post-Compulsory PGCE programme at the Cass School of Education, University of East London. Nina has also authored and edited the QTS Literacy Skills Tests.

Geoff Barker is a professional writer. He was Royal Literary Fund (RLF) Writing Fellow at The University of Dundee (2012-15) and is now RLF Consultant Writing Fellow, providing innovative writing workshops for higher education and secondary schools. Find out more at https://rlfconsultants.com/consultants/geoff-barker/

Contributor

Yasmin Valli is a principal lecturer and Senior Fellow of HEA at Leeds Beckett University. Based in the Carnegie School of Education and Childhood, she has responsibility for newly qualified teachers (NQTs), CPD and Employability. Her main roles are in initial teacher education, across all phases and widening participation. She is also involved in the MA programme and in-service training courses in the field of Educational and Professional Development. Prior to this, she was course leader for the Primary PGCE and OFSTED inspector for the primary and independent sector.

Introduction

Who is this book for?

If you are reading this book it is very likely that you are interested in a teaching career and want to know more about the content of the Professional Skills Tests for trainee teachers and how to pass them. You might currently be a sixth-form or college student considering a Bachelor of Education (BEd) degree, a university student about to finish your subject degree with a view to starting a Postgraduate Certificate in Education (PGCE), or seeking to train as a teacher via one of the many pathways outlined in Chapter 1 of this book. You may already be working in school and seeking to gain QTS through the Assessment Only route or just looking for a change in career. What binds together all readers of this book is the desire to share your expertise with others and to inspire young people with your own enthusiasm for learning.

The good news, whatever your circumstances may be, is that you already have expertise which will stand you in good stead when approaching the skills tests. First and foremost, you will have had active experience, as a pupil or student, of an education system either in the UK or overseas. You already know what it is like to be taught and what it feels like to learn. More on this later, in Chapter 2.

You will probably have read a lot – whether it's fiction, newspapers, business documents or academic papers – and will also have written clearly and accurately on many occasions when studying or at work. All of this will have developed your literacy skills. At this very moment, you will have life experience of budgeting, shopping, balancing your finances or managing a loan. All of these activities call on the numeracy skills assessed in the Professional Skills Tests.

What are the Professional Skills Tests for trainee teachers?

All new entrants to the teaching profession in England, including those on initial teacher training (ITT) and School Direct Programmes, have to pass the skills tests before starting their course leading to the award of Qualified Teacher Status (QTS). The requirement to pass the tests extends to unqualified teachers in schools who are seeking to gain QTS through the Assessment Only route.

The tests cover skills in:

- numeracy, and
- literacy.

The tests are designed to assess whether you can apply these important skills to the degree necessary for their use in your day-to-day work in a school. They are *not* designed to assess whether you have the subject knowledge required to teach English or maths. The tests are taken online by booking a time at a specified centre, are marked instantly and your result – along with feedback on that result – will be given to you before you leave the centre.

You will find more information about the skills tests and the specified centres on the Get Into Teaching website: **https://getintoteaching.education.gov.uk**

How to use this book

The first chapter in this book explores the different routes into teaching. There are a number of different ways to train and this can be confusing for candidates. This chapter helps you to understand the different routes and supports you in choosing which is best suited to your needs. The second chapter looks at teaching and schools, and will help you understand the context of the skills tests and direct you to useful sources where you can conduct your own research into schools and education. Having a familiarity with key terms and issues in education will prove useful when approaching the skills tests and also at a later date when you apply for a training place. Subsequent chapters will outline the content and structure of the literacy and numeracy skills tests and offer you practice questions. Then there is a chapter designed to support your application to teacher training courses and provide suggestions and advice for the interview process. The final chapter 'What is teacher training really like?' offers you real insight into initial teacher training from the point of view of the student and the tutor.

1 | Teacher training and routes into teaching

Yasmin Valli

Teaching remains a popular career choice for many and it continues to attract candidates from a range of backgrounds and expertise. This makes teaching one of the most dynamic and diverse careers that offer clear structure and progression as you move within the profession towards leadership roles. Over the past years, the nature of teacher training has changed considerably, offering teachers-to-be a variety of training routes to enter the teaching profession. This chapter focuses on teacher training routes offered in the UK along with the requirements needed to enter the teaching profession.

(Note that new routes into teaching continue to evolve and any change in policy can influence teacher training. While every effort is made to ensure accuracy, the information in this chapter is subject to any alterations made in the light of changes due to regulations or in policy, including financial and other related items.)

Everyone remembers a good teacher

Your interest in entering the teaching profession may have been sparked off by being inspired by a good teacher, a 'role model' at school, and you may already be aware of the qualities this person had, such as enthusiasm, good subject knowledge, good sense of humour, excellent communications skills, etc. These are some of the desirable qualities for the teaching profession that made them exceptional and made a difference to your schooling. You will develop many of these qualities through your training. From the outset, anyone wanting to teach should set aside some time to engage in research and fact finding to inform their career choice. Guidance is available from government websites and from teacher training providers that will help to shape your decision to enter teaching. In addition to this, you will also be advised to observe and experience classroom settings to get a 'real feel' about teaching and about the desirable qualities and skills needed to become a good teacher. Your training will help you to develop these.

1.1 Eligibility

Make sure that you are eligible to teach before applying for teacher training as different training providers will have specific recruitment criteria. However, there are some basic eligibility requirements you will need to meet to become a teacher. Anyone wanting to teach in England and Wales must complete initial teacher training (ITT). There are a number of different ITT courses available. Before selecting a course, it is important to choose which age you would like to teach. Schooling in England and Wales is divided into four key stages (as stated below) and every teacher must train in at least two key stages:

Key Stage 1 for teaching 3–7-year-old pupils (Primary)
Key Stage 2 for teaching 7–11-year-old pupils (Primary)
Key Stage 3 for teaching 11–14-year-old pupils (Secondary)
Key Stage 4 for teaching 14–16-year-old pupils (Secondary)

1.2 The rewards of teaching

You could receive a substantial tax-free bursary of up to £25,000 (for an update on this figure, check with the Get into Teaching website).

Teachers begin on an average starting salary of £22,900 (£21,588 outside London, £27,000 in London) (for an update on this figure, check with the Get into Teaching website).

Teaching is a highly employable career and prospects of employment in teaching are better than most other professions.

Newly qualified teachers have found teaching jobs in the first 12 months.

Teachers are twice as likely to be in management positions 3.5 years into their career, compared to fellow graduates.

1.3 Qualifications required to teach

Teaching is increasingly a career for the most able graduates. All candidates for teacher training need to have at least a grade C or equivalent in English and maths GCSE. Candidates for primary teaching also need a grade C or equivalent in science. You will need a degree to become a qualified teacher.

If you want to train to teach and obtain qualified teacher status (QTS), you will need to start with the required qualifications to demonstrate your suitability for entry:

- **GCSE grade C or a standard equivalent in mathematics and English to teach at secondary level.**
- **GCSE grade C or a standard equivalent in mathematics, English and a science subject to teach at primary level.**
- **Training providers will also look for at least two A level qualifications in relevant subjects.**
- **For postgraduate teacher training programmes, you will need to hold an undergraduate degree awarded by a higher education provider in England or Wales, or a recognised equivalent qualification.**

Training providers will make the final decision on whether your qualifications meet the entry criteria. If this is not the case, they may ask you to sit a GCSE equivalency test, or ask you to offer other evidence to demonstrate your eligibility for entry.

You will also need to pass the **professional skills test in literacy and numeracy** before your start your training.

For a postgraduate teacher training course, you will need a degree. If your degree subject does not link closely to your chosen teaching subject, you may still be able to apply for a place by undertaking a **subject knowledge enhancement (SKE)** course (see details about SKE in section 1.5 below). The aim of SKE courses is to make teaching an accessible and viable career path to a range of graduates. They are designed to bring a candidate's knowledge of a subject up to secondary teaching level.

Note that you can teach in independent schools, academies and free schools in England without QTS, but it's a definite advantage to have it. Visit the Get Into Teaching website for more information.

If your schooling was outside the UK, then you need to check the National Academic Recognition Information Centre (NARIC) website to find out the equivalency level of your qualifications to UK GCSEs, A levels and an undergraduate degree. If you have non-UK qualifications, you will need a Statement of Comparability from NARIC. This can take some time, so start the process in good time before you submit your application.

If you have overseas equivalent qualifications, you should check your eligibility by contacting your preferred training provider, as they make the final judgement on equivalency.

Professional skills test in literacy and numeracy

It is now a requirement that candidates starting a teacher training course must have passed the professional skills tests in numeracy and literacy before beginning training.

Training providers will use skills tests results to inform decisions during the application process; it is in your interest to pass the tests as soon as possible to increase your chances of success. The skills tests registration system is open for applicants. For details, see the Get Into Teaching website.

Non-academic requirements

Teaching requires you to work with children on a daily basis. It is almost essential to have some experience in an educational setting, although other settings such as after-school clubs, holiday clubs, Brownies, sports clubs, etc. are all good ways of gaining experience. Such experience is good preparation for entry to Initial Teacher Training and most institutions offering teacher training courses require that you show your commitment to a career as a teacher in this way. Therefore, in order to demonstrate your suitability for working with children, you will be required to have up to two weeks' classroom experience before you begin teacher training. It is recommended that you arrange some form of school experience, or you can register and seek help about getting school experience from the Get Into Teaching website.

Medical fitness

Once a training place is accepted, your training provider may send you a health questionnaire to find out about your medical fitness. It is helpful to include information about any disability you have on the application form so that providers can arrange suitable support for you.

Criminal convictions

You will need to disclose any criminal convictions, cautions, or bind-overs, and you will also need to agree to an enhanced criminal record check. It is advisable for you to discuss your circumstances with training providers before you apply.

Disclosure and Barring Service (DBS) in England and Wales

With a strong emphasis on safeguarding, this service enables training providers to identify people who are barred from working with children and vulnerable adults. Check with the DBS to see what you need to do to comply with these arrangements.

Overseas graduates

Graduates from overseas will require a visa. If you're a graduate from overseas, you may need to apply for a visa before starting your teacher training programme. For more information, visit the Get Into Teaching website.

Routes into teaching

Whichever course you choose, you will receive rigorous training and comprehensive guided preparation for your new career. New teachers rate their training as a very good

---

School-led teacher training:

School Direct (salaried/non-salaried)

* School-centred initial teacher training (SCITT)

* Accelerated training programme

University-led teacher training:

* Undergraduate teacher training course (3 or 4 years leading to BEd/BA/BSc Hons degree)

* Postgraduate Certificate in Education (PGCE)

* Subject knowledge enhancement course

Specialist training routes:

Teach First
Researchers in Schools
Assessment Only route
Troops to Teachers
Future teaching scholars
Premier Pathways
Now Teach

We will now consider the various routes as shown in the above diagram.

preparation for the classroom. All courses deliver over 1,000 hours of training. Training input on behaviour management is compulsory.

Before you make up your mind, take a look at the different teacher training routes on offer – this will help with finding the most suitable route for you.

The diagram below identifies the training routes under the different categories that are currently on offer.

1.4 School-led teacher training

For graduates who want the option of hands-on training in a school, the school-led training route(s) are available throughout England. This school-led teacher training route includes some of the country's best schools and allows you the chance to learn on the job in at least two schools, learning from experienced colleagues. Your new skills will be put into practice from day one while you gain qualified teacher status (QTS). Most courses also offer a Postgraduate Certificate in Education (PGCE) through this route. You can apply to train as a teacher with an expectation of a job once you qualify.

With the School Direct Training Programme, you could receive a bursary of up to £20,000 (check the Get Into Teaching website for an update on this figure). With the School Direct Training Programme (salaried) you will be employed by a school and paid a salary.

I selected the school-led teacher training route as I wanted to be in the school environment right from the start. I also wanted to inform my knowledge and understanding about teaching by observing good practice from day one. I was teaching lessons straight away and I gained confidence in the classroom.

(Adam Best, newly qualified teacher)

School Direct

Through this route, schools recruit and train teachers on the job, in partnership with other schools or a university. School Direct courses lead to QTS, possibly a PGCE and/or Master's-level credits. In many cases, School Direct trainees are offered a job in the training school at the end of their training.

The programme takes one year if studied full time and has two approaches:

- School Direct unsalaried – **is available for graduates with a 2:2 or above. As a graduate, you may be eligible for a scholarship/bursary of up to £30,000 to support you during your training (check Get Into Teaching website for an update on this figure)**
- School Direct salaried – **is an employment-based route for graduates with at least three years' work experience. However, some schools may accept applicants with less work experience, especially in maths, physics, chemistry, languages and computing. You will receive an unqualified teacher's salary from your school, and the cost of**

your training will be covered, but you may be charged for your PGCE fees if awarded. Always check with the school you are applying to for more details. Trainees in physics could gain a bursary of up to £30,000 (check the Get Into Teaching website for an update on this figure).

If you are already working at or have an existing relationship with a school and want to take the next step, you may want to consider this route. Trainees on the salaried programme are recruited and employed directly by schools, and often continue teaching in their school following training.

School-centred initial teacher training (SCITT)

If you're a graduate and want to complete your training in a school environment, consider school-centred initial teacher training, which is designed and delivered by groups of neighbouring schools and colleges. Taught by experienced, practising teachers, and often tailored towards local teaching needs, all SCITT courses lead to qualified teacher status (QTS). Many, though not all, will also award you a postgraduate certificate in education (PGCE) validated by a higher education institution.

Accelerated training programme

You now have the opportunity to train on an **accelerated programme**, which is usually over two terms, or part-time over a longer period – usually two years. Accelerated courses offer a full-time intensive training option for highly experienced and skilled individuals capable of achieving qualified teacher status over a shorter period than the standard one year. Completing an accelerated course will typically take two terms, meaning that you could secure a teaching job sooner than on other programmes.

It is recommended that if you are interested in training on an accelerated course, you contact the schools directly before applying. Use the UCAS Teacher Training website to find a programme near you.

1.5 University-led teacher training

Alternatively, you can choose a university-based training course. These courses are provided by training providers in many universities across the UK. You will follow a university training programme which will include time learning in a school. Loans and bursaries are available (check the Get Into Teaching website for an update on financial support).

Many universities offer both undergraduate (three- or four-year course) or a one year postgraduate course leading to qualified teacher status (QTS). Check the appropriate one for you.

Undergraduate teacher training course

This course is taught over three or four years and leads to BA, BEd or BSc Hons degree with QTS. This qualification is ideal for anyone wanting a direct route into teaching in a primary or secondary school after finishing their studies at school or college. This is a particularly popular route into primary school teaching and can include the option of a specialism such as maths. PE with QTS can be offered at secondary level. Make sure you choose an undergraduate course that includes qualified teacher status (QTS) so you can teach in schools. Courses are offered at a number of universities and colleges throughout the UK. Entry requirements may vary from course to course. However, most institutions request a minimum of two A levels or equivalent along with the appropriate GCSEs mentioned above. Contact the course provider to find out more.

Undergraduate routes are usually offered as full-time programmes which take three and four years to complete, but it is also possible to study part-time, which can take up to six years to complete. Whichever option you choose, there will be opportunity to learn from taught modules at university along with a block of periods spent at placement schools throughout the course.

Degrees with opt-in QTS are available in certain subjects such as modern foreign languages, computing and physics. Check the Get Into Teaching website for more details. Applications are generally through UCAS.

> *I enjoyed my teacher training over 3 years at Leeds Beckett University. I wanted to get a real feel about being a teacher by gaining theoretical and practical knowledge. Experience in a variety of placement schools allowed me to connect theory with practice.*
> (Rebecca Smith, primary student on a three-year undergraduate course)

Postgraduate certificate in education (PGCE)

The PGCE is a popular entry path into teaching. It is a one-year course focused on developing your teaching skills and underpinning your knowledge. PGCE is a university-led route leading to QTS. Candidates beginning a PGCE must possess a degree in their chosen subject if they want to teach at secondary level and a relevant degree for teaching if they want to teach at primary level. The PGCE involves a year of postgraduate Initial Teacher Training (ITT). Over the year, a significant amount of training time is spent in schools. Primary trainees spend 18 weeks' school placement in one or two primary schools; secondary trainees spend 24 weeks in secondary schools. The course usually offers taught modules at Master's level and covers teaching techniques, theory and behaviour management.

PGCE courses are available for primary and secondary teaching, and some post-compulsory routes. It will be beneficial to have a good understanding of the age range and/or chosen subject before you start training. A degree in a national curriculum subject is preferred but not essential.

University-led courses are available across England, so there are plenty of options when it comes to location.

Subject knowledge enhancement (SKE) course

Candidates whose degree subject does not link closely to the subject they intend to teach at secondary level are offered SKE to bring their knowledge up to secondary school level. Do not hold back from applying because of your subject knowledge confidence. If you are intending to teach maths, physics, chemistry or modern languages, you could benefit from a subject knowledge enhancement course. Each provider has a different entry requirement, so talk to your chosen provider about your own subject levels. If your provider feels that you would make a good teacher but you need to undertake some additional study in the subject you want to teach before you start training, then your chosen provider can discuss a range of subject knowledge enhancement (SKE) courses available to you. Bursaries are available to candidates on SKE courses, provided you meet the eligibility criteria (check the Get Into Teaching website for more details).

1.6 Specialist training routes

Specialist training options offer different routes to gain QTS depending on your professional or academic background.

Teach First

Teach First is a leadership development programme (LDP) which is supported by partner schools, businesses and universities. It trains its participants to be effective teachers and leaders in schools in low-income areas. Teach First is a charity (England and Wales) that aims to address educational disadvantages by training exceptional teachers to teach in challenging schools. Applicants need to have 300 UCAS points and a 2:1 degree or above, but there is some flexibility with this. The two-year scheme offers an LDP and management skills training for well-qualified graduates. Both primary and secondary trainees gain a Postgraduate Diploma in Education (PGDE – double the credits of a PGCE) with QTS during this two-year period, while working in the classroom and earning a salary.

Applications open in June of the year before you want to start and early application is recommended, especially for popular subjects such as history.

For more information, see the TeachFirst – Graduates website.

Researchers in Schools (RIS): Maths and Physics Chairs programme

The Maths and Physics Chairs programme, part of Researchers in Schools (RIS), is a three-year bespoke, salaried teacher training course for high-calibre candidates who have completed, or are finishing, their PhD. This unique programme offers a combination of classroom teaching and research opportunities, allowing you to develop your skills to become a highly effective classroom teacher – helping all pupils to excel in maths or physics, regardless of background.

Candidates do not pay anything towards their training and all chairs receive a competitive salary while on the programme. Chairs can earn up to £33,900 in year one, rising to up to £38,500 in year two depending on the location (check the Get Into Teaching website for an update on funding).

In addition, you can spend one day per week to pursue the wider aims of the programme and maintain a research profile. The programme starts with an initial summer training module, where you learn the theory of teaching practice and networking with other members of the RIS. After this, you will be placed into a school to develop your teaching practice on the job and work towards gaining qualified teacher status (QTS).

Additional benefits include:

- the opportunity to undertake the Research Leader in Education Award;
- a full teacher's pension;
- an honorary academic position from a research-intensive university;
- a minimum of 10 weeks' paid holiday.

Early applications are strongly encouraged. To find out more and apply, visit the Researchers in Schools website.

Assessment Only (AO) route

Assessment Only (AO) allows you to demonstrate that you already meet all the standards for QTS. So, if you are an experienced teacher with a degree, and have taught for at least two years you can achieve qualified teacher status (QTS) without having to do any further training. To achieve QTS via the AO route, you will need to present detailed evidence to show that you meet the teachers' standards. Your teaching will be assessed in a school by an accredited and approved AO provider. You will also need to take the professional skills test in literacy and numeracy before you can be accepted on to the route. This way of achieving QTS is only available to unqualified teachers who have taught in at least two schools, early years and/or further education settings.

A number of universities, colleges, schools and SCITTs around the country offer AO. Their criteria for entry may vary and you will need to apply to them directly if you are interested in this route to QTS. To find more details, see the Get into Teaching website.

Troops to Teachers

Armed Services leavers can train to teach. If you are interested in teaching secondary maths, biology, chemistry, physics, computing or modern foreign languages, you can fast-track your career into teaching with Troops to Teachers.

Two-year Troops to Teachers courses are for non-graduates and lead to QTS and a degree qualification. This involves:

- earning a salary as an unqualified teacher while you train (this could be 80 per cent of the unqualified teacher pay ranges);
- training to teach in a school for four days a week, with university training one day a week to further your academic qualifications to degree level;
- training in secondary maths, biology, chemistry, physics, computing or modern foreign languages.

For details about eligibility requirements and further information, see the Get Into Teaching website – specialist routes.

Future Teaching Scholars

If you have a passion for maths and physics and are interested in teaching, then the Future Teaching Scholars programme is for you. It offers financial support and is aimed at high-calibre candidates in maths and physics. This six-year programme supports you while you are a maths or physics undergraduate and is followed by specialist teacher training. Taking a maths- or physics-related degree will result in you receiving a £15,000 grant and early preparation for teaching while you study for your degree (check the Get Into Teaching website for an update on funding).

After graduating, you will enter into bespoke employment-based teacher training and earn a salary while you learn your trade. From the outset, you will work in schools and get additional support for two further years. Support will also be available to help you find your first teaching job.

More information is available on the Future Teaching Scholars website.

Premier Pathways

Premier Pathways is school-based teacher training for graduates with a 2:1 or above. You will get paid and in the first year as a trainee you will work as support staff towards becoming an unqualified teacher in Year 2. Participants proceed to complete the course at a school of their choice, graduating with QTS and a PGCE.

Now Teach

If you are considering a career change, then Now Teach can offer a solution. This is a school-based route in London. Trainees study for a PGCE and gain Master's-level credits. They do not need to attend university for any of their training.

1.7 Funding

Funding for Initial Teacher Training is the same as for all other training programmes, including student loans of £9,000 and bursaries for trainees on undergraduate routes.

Trainees on School Direct salaried routes are paid for their teacher training from the beginning.

Trainees on Teach First, some early years teacher programmes and those working in the post-compulsory sector are also paid as they train.

The amount of funding you receive will depend on your academic qualifications, degree classification, the teacher training route you have chosen and your personal circumstances.

Teaching bursaries

Bursaries are offered to graduates as an incentive to teach certain subjects. These non-repayable bursaries of up to £25,000 are available in England. Your entitlement to the bursary will depend on the subject and age range you plan to teach, and your degree classification. It is only available to graduates on a course leading to Qualified Teacher Status (QTS) and if you are not currently employed as a teacher.

For more detailed information on bursaries and scholarships, see:

For England: Get Into Teaching – Bursaries and Funding
For Wales: Teacher Training Wales
For funding in Scotland: Student Awards Agency for Scotland (SAAS)
For funding in Northern Ireland: Student Finance Northern Ireland

Scholarships

Scholarships are competitive. If you have a first or a 2:1 degree, you can apply for a teaching scholarship of up to £30,000, which is available to fund a PGCE in subjects such as physics, maths, chemistry, computing, languages or geography. Scholarships are in partnership with highly regarded professional subject associations. Graduates with experience holding a 2:2 are eligible to apply.

Salaried training

Salaried training is available on the following courses:

Graduate Teacher Programme Wales (GTP)
School Direct salaried route
Early years teacher status (EYTS) graduate employment-based part-time route

Tuition fee loans

Tuition fee loans are paid direct to your university or college. You begin repayment when you are working and earning. The repayment threshold is £21,000 per year.

Professional and Career Development Loans (PCDL)

Students can apply for a **PCDL** three months before the start of their course to receive between £300 and £10,000 for fees and maintenance costs. You must have been resident in the UK for three years prior to starting the course and plan to work in the UK/EU after the course. Competition can be fierce, so you need to apply as early as possible.

Disabled Students' Allowance (DSA)

DSA supports you with additional funding and provides for the extra costs towards your training due to your disability. It does not have to be repaid and is not assessed around your household income. Find out more about **disability-related funding**.

1.8 Applying for teacher training

A degree and a recognised teaching qualification are required if you want to teach in a UK state school. However, you will need to continue seeking updates on the requirements and qualifications as new routes into teaching emerge. You also need to decide where you plan to train and teach as the routes, entry requirements and statutory teaching standards are different. You can apply through UCAS for the main postgraduate and undergraduate teacher training programmes in England, Wales and Scotland.

For teacher training routes in the UK, it is essential to forward a completed application form along with a personal statement. By this time you will have researched the training route you intend to follow along with the age range and the subject you wish to study. You also need to include your school experience and ensure that your qualifications are in line with the entry requirements. Go to events and open days to find out more about your route and to seek further clarification. All this will help you with your application.

Before completing your application form and personal statement, you need to think through all the information carefully as your application will act as 'first impressions', so try to make it count. Check for spelling and grammar mistakes, too.

For references, you need to ensure that the person(s) whose name(s) you forward are able to support your application appropriately and comment on your suitability to teach. It is useful to seek a reference from the school where you carried out your experience. Remember that your application will go through first and second sort to ensure that you meet the entry criteria before a decision is made to invite you to an interview.

For guidance on applications and personal statements, visit the UCAS Teaching in the UK website.

1.9 Interviews

Successful applications result in interviews. The interview will give you the opportunity to show that you possess the skills and qualities required for the teaching profession. Many institutions include small interview tasks for you to complete either in groups or individually. This is when they observe your suitability for selection in line with the criteria. There is usually a chance to include a brief one-to-one interview with training providers, during which further questions are asked to assess your suitability for the selected route.

At the interview, be prepared to articulate your school experience with confidence and give examples to support your responses. Some questions will test your awareness about the wider educational matters and current issues in education, so do your preparation well. Most institutions will give you information about the interview day, which will help with your preparation.

Try the Get Into Teaching interactive interview and application assistant for further tips on interviews.

Useful websites

Get Into Teaching: https://getintoteaching.education.gov.uk/explore-my-options/teacher-training-routes

UCAS: www.ucas.com/teaching-in-the-uk

2 | It's all about teaching and schools

The importance of literacy and numeracy skills

The professional skills tests... for prospective teachers assess the core skills that teachers need to fulfil their professional role in schools, rather than the subject knowledge needed for teaching. This is to ensure all teachers are competent in numeracy and literacy, regardless of their specialism.

(Department for Education, 2017)

In other words, while all teachers need to be confident in the subject matter they are teaching, they also need to be highly proficient users of English and mathematics. As professionals, teachers work not only with their own pupils but also with other members of the school community including teacher colleagues, classroom assistants, parents and governors. In addition, a teacher's role often requires liaising with external individuals and organisations such as inspectors, health workers, charities, social services, education advisors and visiting speakers, all of whom will look for professional competence. And this 'professional competence' includes the ability to communicate effectively and to work successfully with numbers.

English and maths are essential life-skills, and English language and Mathematics GCSEs are a vital key to young people's progression onto further education and employment. With this in mind, teachers across all levels and subjects share the responsibility for equipping themselves with the necessary skills to help support their pupils on this journey.

How will these skills help me in my teaching career?

As a primary school teacher your timetable will include 'stand-alone' lessons in English and maths where you will be helping to develop the knowledge and confidence of your pupils. Your training course will provide plenty of input to help you understand how children learn, as well as the fundamentals of 'best practice' when teaching these subjects. However, the responsibility for your pupils' literacy and numeracy does not lie solely within these timetabled lessons. As a prospective secondary school teacher whose specialism is not English or maths, the classroom application of these skills may not seem immediately obvious. So for both primary and secondary teachers, here are just a few examples of occasions when awareness of both maths and English are important to a professional teacher's working life:

Classroom teaching:
- creating worksheets and handouts for your pupils;
- labelling displays for classrooms or corridors;
- writing directly onto the board during a lesson;
- providing clear and precise explanations;
- calculating timing in order to maintain pace and cover a topic in a lesson;

- marking pupils' work and homework and providing written feedback or numerical totals;
- calculating proportions for mixing paints or materials, or for allocating resources for creative activities;
- explaining to pupils the breakdown of grading elements in public exams;
- presenting background or historical information chronologically.

Administration:
- constructing clear, timed lesson plans;
- sending clear and succinct emails;
- writing notices or leaflets for notice boards;
- producing internal reports on the outcome of curriculum initiatives;
- researching and filling in 'risk assessment' forms for trips;
- using management information systems;
- budgeting e.g. for consumable resources or trips;
- target setting, using statistics based on pupils' prior achievement;
- compiling, using and analysing statistics such as attendance figures or exam results.

External liaison:
- writing letters or notices for parents/carers;
- composing progress reports for pupils and their parents/carers;
- compiling information and liaising with other professionals such as health workers or educational psychologists;
- working with the Parent Teacher Association on planning and funding events;
- liaising by phone or email with outside speakers;
- devising a schedule and handling money for trips.

Continuing professional development (CPD) and scholarly activity:
- sharing best practice with colleagues – using evidence from your own teaching;
- communicating clearly, taking notes and feeding back effectively when attending CPD at school or elsewhere;
- conducting practitioner research on both your own and your colleagues' classroom practice;
- writing articles for a wider audience e.g. teaching magazines, educational journals;
- pursuing a Masters or PhD programme.

Doing your homework

What do I need to know about teaching?

The skills tests... are set in the context of the professional role of a teacher [and] assess the use of real data and information which teachers are likely to encounter...

(Department for Education, 2017)

Depending on your experiences to date, the Department for Education information above may come as a pleasant confirmation of your expectations. Or it may provoke a sense of uncertainty and unease. Whichever applies to you, the next section of this book is designed to provide a guide to easily accessible sources which will help you familiarise yourself with typical educational contexts and 'education-specific' language. Of course you can usefully draw on your general knowledge, everyday reading and common sense, but the sources below will also introduce you to topical issues and debates in education, explored from a variety of perspectives. Not only will this research support your preparation for the skills tests, but it will also help you get ready for your teacher training applications and interviews.

As you are researching, it may be useful to create a glossary of *key terms* and their meanings. If you cannot work out the meaning of a word from its context, look at the *Talking to teachers* section below for suggestions of how to find out first-hand. Alternatively, you could use one of the glossaries available online e.g. **www.nga.org.uk/Guidance/Glossary.aspx** but watch out for the non-UK glossaries which have an entirely different lexicon!

In the meantime, here are some terms which you might find useful.

Term	Definition
Assessment	An activity (e.g. a test, quiz, game, question and answer, piece of writing) which seeks to measure a pupil's knowledge, progress or attainment.
Assignment	A piece of work which a trainee teacher or pupil must complete – usually within a given time-frame and for the purpose of assessment.
Benchmark	An existing point of reference against which attainment (e.g. pupil test scores, school exam results) can be measured.
Curriculum	The set of 'courses of study' offered by a school. In primary and secondary schools this is largely determined by the National Curriculum – see below.
Dyslexia	A disorder (sometimes called a 'specific learning difficulty') which affects the ability to learn to read but does not affect general intelligence.
E-learning	A term which describes any learning which makes use of new technologies such as email, internet, online discussion forums, mobile devices, etc.
Interactive whiteboard	A display board connected to a computer and a projector, and used as a classroom teaching tool.
Key Stages	The stages of school pupils' education to which elements of the National Curriculum (see below) apply: • Key Stage 1 (KS1) Years 1–2 age 5–7 • Key Stage 2 (KS2) Years 3–6 age 7–11 • Key Stage 3 (KS3) Years 7–9 age 11–14 • Key Stage 4 (KS4) Years 10–11 age 14–16
National Curriculum	A programme of study, set by the government, which outlines what pupils need to study at each Key Stage and sets attainment targets.
Phonics	A strategy for teaching reading, based on letter-sound relationships.
Pupil-teacher ratio	The number of pupils in a school divided by the number of full-time teachers.
Reading age	A pupil's level of reading ability as compared to the average age at which a comparable ability is found.

Term	Definition
SATs	Standard Assessment Tasks. These are tests taken by pupils at the end of each Key Stage in order to assess progress against the National Curriculum.
Safeguarding	Actions or policies adopted by an institution in order to promote the welfare of, prevent harm to, and protect children or vulnerable adults.
Special educational needs	Physical disabilities or learning difficulties which make it harder for children to access education and/or learn.
Supply teacher	A teacher who is employed to cover for an absent teacher or a temporary vacancy in a school.
Syllabus	An outline of the contents of a course of study.
Target setting	The practice of setting a level of performance expected of a pupil, department or school.
Year group	The grouping of students by age – see 'National Curriculum' above.

Another thing you might notice while conducting preparatory research into schools is the frequent use of acronyms. Here are some common and useful ones to learn and explore further.

Acronym	Meaning
AfL	Assessment for Learning
APP	Assessment of Pupil Progress
BME	Black and Minority Ethnic
CPD	Continuing Professional Development
DBS	Disclosure and Barring Service
DDA	Disability Discrimination Act
E&D	Equality and Diversity
EAL	English as an Additional Language
ECM	Every Child Matters
EO	Equal Opportunities
ESOL	English for Speakers of Other Languages
EWO	Education Welfare Officer
EYFS	Early Years Foundation Stage
FE	Further Education
G&T	Gifted and Talented
GCSE	General Certificate of Secondary Education
H&S	Health and Safety
HMI	Her Majesty's Inspector(ate)
HoD	Head of Department

Acronym	Meaning
HoY	Head of Year
ICT	Information and Communication Technology
INSET	In-Service Training
ITE	Initial Teacher Education
ITT	Initial Teacher Training
KS	Key Stage
LA	Local Authority
LSA	Learning Support Assistant
MIS	Management Information System
NCTL	National College for Teaching and Leadership
NQT	Newly Qualified Teacher
NRA	National Record of Achievement
OfSTED	Office for Standards in Education
PSHE	Personal, Social, Health and Economic Education
PTA	Parent Teacher Association
QTS	Qualified Teacher Status
SENCO	Special Educational Needs Co-ordinator
SENDA	Special Educational Needs Discrimination Act
SLDD	Specific Learning Difficulties and/or Disabilities
SMT	Senior Management Team
TA	Teaching Assistant
UCAS	Universities and Colleges Admissions Service
Y1, Y2 etc.	Year 1, Year 2

Online information sources

There are numerous places online where you can start your research into schools and teaching. These range from the more formal and 'official' websites outlining government regulations and legislation, to less formal sites which encourage question and debate on educational issues. There are also websites which offer teaching tips and resources or provide a forum for teachers to share ideas and experiences. Below is a list of sites worth browsing, but as you explore these you may well come across others to bookmark for future use.

- **Department for Education (DfE)**
  https://www.gov.uk/government/organisations/department-for-education
  This is the 'official' website where you can access information on government policy and strategy. There are links to articles and data, as well as a link from the home page to the DfE *Get Into Teaching* pages.

- **Get Into Teaching** – *www.education.gov.uk/get-into-teaching*
  Here you will find all the important information about getting into teaching, including applications, bursaries, salaries and Professional Skills Tests. A very useful resource!
- **Local Authority/Council websites**
  Each local authority, city or county council has its own website. Here you will find a link from the home page to information on local education provision, designed for residents within the local area. This is generally factual information, presented in a form which the general public can understand.
- **Legislation.gov.uk** – *www.legislation.gov.uk*
  On this government website you will be able to search under 'education' to find current and past legislation. As you would expect, this is written in fairly complex and legalistic language.

Newspapers and magazines

- **The *Times Educational Supplement* (TES)**
  The TES is a well-regarded weekly publication (in magazine format) specifically designed for teachers and those interested in education. It includes articles and features on UK and international education as well as reviews and lesson ideas. There is also free online access to the TES website *www.tes.co.uk* where you can find teaching resources, teaching forums and a comprehensive jobs section.
- **The *Guardian***
  The *Guardian* newspaper has an education section every Tuesday covering all stages of education from Early Years to Higher Education. Articles are accessible and include personal opinions from educationalists as well as journalists. These articles can also be accessed by going to the *Guardian* online at *www.theguardian.com/education*. In addition, there is a connected *Guardian* 'Teacher Network' site *www.theguardian.com/teacher-network* where teachers can share resources and participate in discussions on the Teacher Network blog. There is plenty here of interest to non- or beginning-teachers.

Subject associations

If you are teaching a particular subject e.g. English or maths, there is likely to be a national organisation to promote teaching excellence in your field. This will offer a space where you can share ideas, views and resources with colleagues. Here are a few, but you can try searching for others by using the search phrase 'association for *[your subject]*'.

- **National Association for the Teaching of English (NATE)** – *www.nate.org.uk*
- **Association of Teachers of Mathematics (ATM)** – *www.atm.org.uk*
- **Association for Science Education** – *www.ase.org.uk/home*
- **Association for Language Learning** – *www.all-languages.org.uk*
- **Association for Citizenship Teaching (ACT)** – *www.teachingcitizenship.org.uk*
- **Personal, Social, Health and Economic Education Association** – *www.pshe-association.org.uk*
- **Music Mark** – *www.musicmark.org.uk*

Unions and teaching associations

The major teaching unions all have members' websites which offer information on legislation, campaigns, pay and conditions, benefits and training. They also have magazines which are available in hard copy and/or online to their members who are encouraged to participate in discussions via Facebook or Twitter.

- National Union of Teachers (NUT) – *www.teachers.org.uk*
  Magazine – *The Teacher*
- National Association of Schoolmasters Union of Women Teachers (NASUWT) – *www.nasuwt.org.uk*
  Magazine – *Teaching Today*
- Association of Teachers and Lecturers (ATL) – *www.atl.org.uk*
  Magazine – *Report*

Other websites

In addition to the above websites, there are several which offer an insight into different aspects of education. Here are a few of the most useful ones:

- BBC News: Education and Family – *www.bbc.co.uk/news/education/*
  News stories, videos, feature articles and analysis.
- BBC Learning – *www.bbc.co.uk/learning/*
  A well laid-out and accessible site (archived) with information and resources designed for students, parents and teachers.
- BBC iwonder - *www.bbc.co.uk/iwonder*
  An attractive and accessible website (archived) with information on 'big questions' in different curricular areas.
- Oxfam Education – *www.oxfam.org.uk/education/*
  A readable site which focuses on 'global citizenship' information, resources and activities for schools.

There are many teaching resources websites on the internet, both general and subject-specific, and browsing these will give you an idea of the types of materials used by many teachers. Some require you to register before using the site but most have free access to lesson plans and materials. Practising teachers make use of these sites to upload and share their own materials and to benefit from the good practice of others. Examples include:

- www.teachingideas.co.uk
- www.primaryresources.co.uk
- www.teachit.co.uk
- www.teachitprimary.co.uk
- www.bbc.co.uk/education
- Teachers TV
  Despite its name, this bank of resources for teachers (previously viewed on the Teachers TV channel) is now available only online. It comprises a huge collection of broadcast-quality videos covering all aspects of schools and teaching, including CPD, whole school issues, job roles in schools and the teaching of a wide range of curriculum levels and subjects. The materials can be accessed via several websites but are help-fully listed and categorised on *www.proteachersvideo.com*

Talking to teachers

Using real teachers as a resource

If you want to find out more about schools and teaching, who could be better placed to provide this information than someone who is already a teacher? Classroom teachers are an excellent resource. They are on-the-job and will be able to answer your questions using their experience, with illustrative examples and anecdotes. They can also provide valuable tips for skills tests, applications and interviews.

Think about the opportunities to ask questions which draw out the type of information that might be harder to find in more formal settings:

- What made you choose this career?
- What is the best thing about your job?
- What is the hardest thing about teaching?
- Have you got any good techniques for preparing for the skills tests?
- How can I prepare for my teacher training course interview?
- What is most useful to know before I start my training course?
- What is your number-one piece of advice to a prospective trainee teacher?

Teacher friends and family
Do you know anyone personally who has recently qualified as a teacher? Would they be prepared to spend some time with you to work through some of your questions and give you the benefit of their experience?

School visits and placements
Many teacher training institutions insist that all trainees spend time in a school before they start their course. They may give you guidance on how to find a placement. However, even where this is not compulsory, it is strongly recommended. There is no substitute for spending a period of time observing what goes on in the classroom and, if possible, 'behind the scenes' in the staff-room and at staff meetings. If you get this opportunity, try to speak to as many people as possible. Bear in mind that everyone in a school will have timetables to observe and deadlines to meet, so pick the right time to approach them. Head teachers, deputies, senior managers, classroom teachers, teaching assistants, classroom technicians (e.g. in science, technology or art) and mid-day supervisors can all provide an important perspective on the part education plays in the lives of the pupils in the school.

Although visiting a school may seem daunting at first, you will soon find that you pick up the jargon and begin to get a feel for how the institution is organised. If you are making a one-day visit, you will probably just observe what is going on and make a mental note of any questions you would like to ask should you get the chance. If you are fortunate enough to spend longer in the school then you could try to gain a more comprehensive picture of the institution and the work of the staff. Below are some suggested questions designed to help you gain a deeper understanding of what you are observing.

Questions for school managers
- How is the school day organised? Why?
- What safeguarding measures are in place for pupils and staff?
- How does the school promote equality of opportunity and inclusion for all pupils?
- What kind of special educational needs do pupils in this school have? How are these catered for?
- What qualities do you look for in beginner-teachers?

Can you think of any other important questions you'd like to ask a school manager?

Questions for classroom teachers

Try to sit in on some lessons and then ask the teacher about how they planned for that lesson.

- Why is the classroom laid out in this way?
- What did you want the pupils to learn by the end of the lesson?
- Why did you choose certain activities and organise them in that particular order?
- What decisions did you have to make during the lesson? Why?
- Why did you choose the resources you used today?
- How did you check that all the pupils were learning?

Again, what would you really like to know about teaching? Think of three more questions to ask a classroom teacher.

Arranging a school visit

While schools are extremely busy places, many institutions welcome people who are interested in becoming a teacher and will do their best to accommodate you and answer your questions. Depending on your circumstances, visits can be arranged in a variety of ways, but do check the regulations regarding Disclosure and Barring Service (DBS) checks before you visit.

Your own school

Try getting in touch with teachers from your old primary or secondary school. They may be able to make a formal arrangement for you to come and spend some time shadowing them. If you are still attending secondary school, and thinking about applying for a teaching degree, you could ask to sit in on lessons with some of the younger pupils. See if you can help out in the classroom.

Your child's school

If you have a child in school, particularly in a primary school, the head teacher may be pleased to invite you in as a volunteer to assist on a regular basis with reading or other classroom activities.

A local school

If you are an undergraduate or graduate hoping to teach in a secondary school, you can apply to join the School Experience Programme. Find out more on the Get Into Teaching website at **https://getintoteaching.education.gov.uk/school-experience**

If you want to arrange your own school experience, you can use your local authority website (see above) or search via the EduBase portal **www.education.gov.uk/edubase** to find a list of schools in your area. Ring up to find out who is the most suitable person to speak to (for example the person in charge of Teaching and Learning) and then send an email directly to that person explaining your position. Do try to be flexible with visiting dates though, as there are certain times of year when schools are particularly busy. Even better, if you are able to offer your services as a volunteer, your visit will benefit not just you but the school as well.

Making the most of your own experience

What experiences do I already have?

If you are thinking about becoming a teacher, you may well already have taken part in activities which have inspired your decision. These may have helped you to focus on a particular age group. Teaching and learning doesn't just happen in formal classrooms and any experience of motivating pupils is good preparation for your future career.

Here are some typical ways in which prospective trainee teachers work with children, young people or peers before applying for their training course. If you have not yet had an opportunity to teach, some of the activities suggested below may be accessible to you:

- volunteering on youth projects or summer play schemes;
- helping younger pupils in your school with their reading or maths;
- helping out in your own child's school e.g. with classroom activities, school events or trips;
- becoming a mentor or 'study buddy' to local school pupils while doing your degree;
- leading study groups or seminars at university;
- informally tutoring family and friends;
- childminding, babysitting or looking after children;
- gap-year activities such as volunteering overseas or teaching English as a Foreign Language (EFL);
- community volunteering e.g. through Community Service Volunteers (CSV);
- volunteering to work with children in a local community group or in a religious organisation such as a church or mosque;
- employment as a classroom assistant;
- working as a youth leader in an organisation such as Scouts, Guides or Woodcraft Folk;
- supporting school students on work experience in your own workplace;
- mentoring new colleagues or running training sessions in your place of employment.

How can I use my experience?

Experience in teaching contexts will certainly help to develop your familiarity with the skills tests scenarios, but that is not the only benefit. The ability to discuss your thoughts on what makes a good learning experience will also give you more confidence in interviews and impress your interviewer. If you have not yet been a 'teacher' then you will certainly have been a student or 'learner' at several points in your life. This experience will provide you with answers to some of the crucial questions you will need to ask yourself as you become an educator. Whatever the age of their pupils or the subject they are teaching, a teacher's single most important question is always: 'Are my pupils learning?'

A useful exercise

Now – get out a pen and large piece of paper, or open up a blank document on your computer. Give yourself up to half an hour to complete all the questions below. Answer the questions as fully and honestly as possible. Perhaps answer in note form at first and, if you have the time, write it up in full. It's a good literacy exercise, too.

- How would you define 'teaching'?
- How would you define 'learning'?
- What was your best experience as a learner?
- What was your worst experience as a learner?
- What did the teacher do to make the experience good or bad?
- What do good teachers do to help their students learn?
- What attitudes do you think these good teachers have towards their learners?
- What lessons or conclusions about teaching can you draw from the answers to the questions above?

What's the point?

By answering the above questions, did you feel you started to think more critically about your own unique experiences as a student or learner? Did you consider the very nature of teaching and learning? How important is teaching to you personally? Are you motivated to pursue a career in teaching?

Reference

Department for Education, 2017. *Professional Skills Test*. Available at: http://sta.education.gov.uk [Accessed 14 October 2017].

3 | The Literacy Skills Test

3.1 Introduction

You need to pass a test of your own literacy skills before you can be admitted to a course of teacher education. This applies to all candidates, whether you see yourselves as having an English specialism or not. This book is designed to help you to pass that test. The necessary knowledge is explained, examples of questions are provided and answers to those questions are supplied, along with *Key points* to indicate the main things that need attention.

The areas covered in the book – spelling, punctuation, grammar and comprehension – are the ones that appear in the test. The particular aspects of spelling, etc., are also the ones that are in the test. The actual form of the questions is also similar. Everything you will be tested on is explained; examples are given and the questions give you plenty of practice for the test. The questions in the test will be a selection from the types of question shown here in each section.

Why is the knowledge of English of intending teachers being tested?

Teachers need to have a confident knowledge of English. A teacher who has a sound idea of how the English language is organised can help children to use it well. Some approaches – especially guided writing – can only be successful if the teacher knows, for example, what it is about a child's writing that makes it good and also knows how it could be improved.

Teachers receive a great deal of written information and have to be able to understand it and act on it with assurance. They often have to write, or collaborate in writing, documents such as school policies, reports on their children, information for parents, etc.

Teachers and their use of English are very much in the public eye. Parents, governors, inspectors and others see them in their professional role and, inevitably, make judgements. Teachers need to know enough and be competent enough to deal confidently with the world they move in.

Finally, the right of children to be taught by somebody who knows enough about English to be able to help them is the basis of the test and of this book.

What is the test like?

The test will be carried out online. For the spelling test, you will use headphones (multiple-choice spelling options will be available for candidates with hearing impairment). The test has four sections: Spelling, Punctuation, Grammar and Comprehension.

You will be asked to:

- **type in or select your answers for Spelling;**
- **type in or delete and amend characters for Punctuation;**
- **drag and drop multiple-choice options into text for Grammar;**
- **drag and drop options in order to: match statements to categories; complete a list; sequence information; identify points; match text to summaries; identify meaning of words/phrases; evaluate statements; select headings; and identify readership for Comprehension.**

You will not be tested on the National Curriculum nor on how to teach English. You will be tested on four main sections of knowledge about literacy: Spelling, Punctuation, Grammar and Comprehension.

The Spelling section of the test *has* to be attempted first. Once the Spelling section is done, you must go on to the other sections and cannot return to Spelling. There is no restriction on how you go about the other three sections. You can do them in any order; tackle questions within each section in any order; and move about within each section as much as you like. It may make more sense to do the Grammar test last but that is up to you.

In the Literacy Skills Test, each test has a unique pass mark, dependent on the questions that are included. The total number of marks available for each test varies from 45 to 49, again dependent on the questions that are included. Spelling has a total of 10 marks, Punctuation 15, Grammar 10–12 and Comprehension 10–12. If, as is likely, the test has 48 questions, 31 correct answers can gain you a pass.

This is what the four sections cover and how they are approached in the test:

Spelling

Teachers are expected to spell correctly. That includes the words that are likely to appear in their professional work. The emphasis on correct spelling is justified because it avoids ambiguity (for example, advise/advice; affect/effect) and is easier to read than incorrect spelling. In the test, you are expected to use British English spelling but either *-ize* or *-ise* verb endings will be allowed.

You will need to wear headphones for this part of the computerised test. You will see ten sentences on the screen. One word has been deleted from each sentence. Where a word has been deleted, there appears an icon for *Audio* . When you reach that word in your reading, click the icon and listen through your headphones. You will hear the deleted word. Decide how you think it is spelled and type your decision directly into the box provided in the deletion space. If you need to have the word repeated, click the audio icon again. You can do this as many times as you want, even if you are only part of the way through spelling the word, or have finished and just want to check. You may also make several attempts to spell a word but you should keep in mind that the whole test allows only about 45 minutes.

A multiple-choice spelling option is available for candidates with hearing impairment. As this is a book, not a computer, the practice questions follow the same rubric and format as the hearing impaired multiple-choice questions in the Literacy Skills Test:

Select the correctly spelled word from the box of alternatives. Write your answer in the space in the sentence.

1   As I had used the school's petty cash to buy some materials, I kept all the _____ to give to the head.

receipts
receits
reciepts
reciets

2   Teachers used their _____ judgement when selecting topics for discussion.

professional
proffesional
profesional
professionel

Punctuation

Teachers are expected to be able to read and use punctuation correctly, especially in those texts that they are likely to encounter or to produce as part of their professional work. Punctuation that is consistent and that follows the conventions makes a text easy to read. Errors in punctuation not only give a reader more work to do but can also change the meaning or create ambiguity in the text. They can also create a bad impression, especially if the error is caused through obvious carelessness. Knowing what punctuation is needed, and where it should go, reveals both an awareness of the reader's needs and, fundamentally, a high degree of literacy.

Unlike spelling, there is a personal element in punctuation. By the time you have finished the book, you might have noticed that we use more semicolons than most people.

Many writers never use semicolons at all. The point is that, if they are used, they should be used consistently.

The point about consistency is such a key one that it is worth considering it here. Suppose you have written this sentence:

My early experience with the class has led me to modify my medium-term plans.

Now suppose that you want to add something to that sentence to express, however mildly, your feelings about having to make the changes. You decide to add the word *unfortunately.* That word can go at the beginning of the sentence (with a comma immediately after it) or at the end (with a comma immediately before it) or in the middle, between *me* and *to.* That is an interruption in the grammatical structure of the sentence and such interruptions are marked by commas. A common failing is to put just one comma, either before or after the interruption, but you actually need two, one before and one after the interruption, like this:

My early experience with the class has led me, unfortunately, to modify my medium-term plans.

Consistency means that you do not put just one comma in this case but that you use both. They are partners.

The test is presented online. You will see a text that has some punctuation omitted. Your task is to identify where to place a punctuation mark, change a lower case letter to an upper case one or create a new paragraph. When you have decided what change to make, double click on the word you have chosen to edit – the word before the punctuation mark – and a dialogue box will appear. The word you clicked will appear in a box. Type in your punctuation and click OK. The box will disappear and the word and your punctuation choice will appear in the text but will now be blue. To add a new paragraph, double click on the word before the new paragraph is to begin, click on the letter 'P' which is in the dialogue box and click OK. You can change your answer if you think you should.

Sometimes, although it is possible to insert a punctuation mark, it may not be necessary or even appropriate. You have to decide. What is very important is that you create a text whose punctuation is wholly consistent. Your criterion is to ask yourself what would be *consistent with the punctuation in the text.* Remember to add up your changes so that they total 15 and also remember there are only 15 correct amendments. If you insert punctuation where it is correct but not necessary, it will not add to your score nor will any marks be deducted.

This is the sort of question you are likely to meet in the book. As this is a book, not a computer, you cannot type in your chosen punctuation mark; instead, you simply note which punctuation mark or other change in punctuation is necessary at which point to make the whole consistent. There will be passages like this for you to practise your knowledge of punctuation; your job is to make it appropriate and consistent in its use of punctuation:

although the literacy framework had been working well some staff wondered how to maintain the good work they had done in other areas of the curriculum could drama and pe be retained at the same level as previously

Grammar

Teachers need to be able to see whether a piece of writing is, or is not, in Standard English, the variety of English that is required in formal texts and, therefore, in almost all writing. They also need to be able to say if the text makes sense and, if not, what prevents it from making sense. Finally, they need to be aware of the style that is appropriate to a particular type of text and to understand what, if anything, is wrong with the style.

The test is multiple-choice. You will see a passage that is not quite complete; bits of language are missing. The decision about what should be inserted to complete the passage is a grammatical choice. You will be shown a range of possible bits of language to insert, only one of which would complete that part of the passage satisfactorily. The choice of that insertion will depend on your reading the whole passage carefully as well as the sentence that has to be completed. You insert your choice simply by dragging it into position.

Below is an example of a sentence that is incomplete. Four possible ways of completing the sentence are offered. Your task is to choose the one that fits grammatically:

The assembly focussed on the current playground incidents

Now choose one of the following to complete the sentence:

a. *that were making life difficult for the infants.*
b. *that was making life difficult for the infants.*
c. *that are making life difficult for the infants.*
d. *that is making life difficult for the infants.*

Comprehension

Teachers receive a good deal of written material that they must understand and to which they must respond. This test puts an emphasis on close, analytical reading of a passage of text. You will need to read the passage with attention to the main ideas, with an awareness of its arguments and, sometimes, with an idea of how it affects your existing ideas. You might need to make judgements about the text and to organise and reorganise its content. Since that is what being a teacher now involves, the test assesses your ability to read in this way.

The comprehension test uses a range of multiple-choice style questions. You will be expected to drag and drop selected options in order to:

- match statements to categories;
- complete a list;
- sequence information;
- identify points;
- match text to summaries;
- identify meaning of words/phrases;
- evaluate statements;
- select headings;
- identify readership.

The test will present you with the sorts of text that teachers are likely to see and read as part of their professional lives. You will be expected to identify key points, read between the lines, tell fact from fiction, make judgements, etc. Not every test will examine every aspect!

At its simplest, the test might ask you to identify the meaning of words and phrases. Remember that no one test will test every aspect of every one of the four sections. In the following short passage, for example, you are asked to identify from a given list of options who you think is the intended audience for the text:

> *You will have seen from the local press, where results are published from every school in the Authority, that this school has had a consistently high standard of performance in the annual SATs over several years. This fine record is expected to continue for some years, at least. A consequence of this success is that the school is oversubscribed each year and, regretfully, it is not always possible to offer a place to every child whose parents apply to us.*

How to prepare for the test

- Use this chapter to get a good grasp of what understanding is demanded by the test.
- Go to the DfE website (www.education.gov.uk/sta/professional/b00211208/literacy) to read their advice, familiarise yourself with the test and what it looks like, and try the practice tests.
- From that practice, identify which areas you need to improve on and refer to this book.
- Remember that doing well in spelling and punctuation can take you close to the pass mark.
- Read again the Hints in each section of this chapter.

How to use this chapter

For the purposes of the test, literacy is seen as comprising the four topics detailed above: Spelling, Punctuation, Grammar and Comprehension; each of which has its own section in this chapter. There you will find an explanation of the knowledge required, examples of the features of literacy being tested and explicit direction about what to do in the test. There are practice questions for each section. Answers to the practice questions are provided in section 3.6.

Revision checklist

The following chart shows in detail the coverage of the four main sections. You can use the checklist in your revision to make sure that you have covered all the key content areas.

Professional suitability and style	Pages
Non-parallelism in lists	78
Inconsistent register and tone	79
Shift in person within sentences or across sentences	80
Redundancy/tautology	82
Inappropriate conjunctions	82
COMPREHENSION	
Attributing statements to categories	90
Completing a bulleted list	90
Sequencing information	91
Presenting main points	91
Matching texts to summaries	92
Identifying the meanings of words and phrases	92
Evaluating statements about the text	93
Selecting headings and sub-headings	94
Identifying possible readership or audience for a text	94

3.2 Spelling

Introduction

10 marks are available for spelling.

If you want to write well, good spelling is not as important as good grammar or even good punctuation but it is still important. Some great writers have been poor spellers; some bad writers can spell any word they need.

Correct spelling is not a mark of intelligence but it is very helpful to a reader because poor spelling interferes with the flow of easy reading. If a text is correctly written, the good spellings will not be noticed because all the reader's attention has gone straight to the meaning. Ideally, when someone reads what you write, they should be able to pay attention to what you want to say, to your meaning, and not be distracted by poor spelling. Bad spelling interferes with the reader's attention just as a fault in glass can interfere with the view through a window.

There are no tricks in the test; you will not have to learn how to spell *phthisis* especially for the occasion. If you can spell the kinds of word that are in common use, especially in the world of education, you will have no problems. British spelling rather than American is expected although either *-ise* or *-ize* at the ends of some verbs is acceptable. However, be consistent in your use of whichever you choose.

The actual form of the test is described in the Introduction. For the practice questions in this section (see pages 40–45), a number of sentences are presented, with one word deleted each time. A box below the sentence contains four alternative spellings of the missing word. Complete the sentence by writing in the correct spelling of the missing word.

Essential knowledge

The commonest spelling problem for adults, even educated and well-read adults, is when to use a **double consonant,** as in:

accommodation	exaggerate	harass
committee	success	assess
professional	apprentice	misspell
disappoint	innumerable	

Unfortunately, there is no easy way to remember them. They have to be learned by heart. What does help is simply to write a good deal. If you are in the habit of writing, even brief notes to yourself to help you to think through an issue, all aspects of your writing (with the probable exception of handwriting!) will improve. As with so much in life, use it or lose it.

It does help you if you notice those words that you know give you trouble. Look at the following list of some double-consonant words and copy out any that you suspect have been problems for you in the past. When you have a list, look at each word in turn, remember the *whole word*, its sequences of letters, its prefix and suffix (if any), and try to write it again. Then check it.

abbreviate	immeasurable
acclimatise	(in)efficient
address	millennium
allowed	miscellaneous
apparent	miscellany
appear	necessary
apprentice	occur/occurred
approach	occurrence
appropriate	omit/omission
approve	opportunity
approximate	parallel
assess	passage
challenge	permissible
commensurate	permission
commit/committed	possess
correspondence	proceed (but precede)
correspondent	questionnaire
curriculum	recommend
disappear	recur/recurrence
dissipate	satellite
embarrass	succeed
exaggerate	success
excellent	succinct
grammar	terrible
grip/gripped	truthfully
happily	till (but until)
harass	vacillate

There is a special category of words with double consonants. Some stem words, like *fulfil* in *fulfilling*, end in a single consonant – that is, a vowel and a consonant – but then double the final consonant if either *-ed* or *-ng* is added. Some other words in this category are:

commit   *begin*

Note: Benefit, benefited *are exceptions.*

Remarkably, since spelling is normally either right or wrong, you are allowed two choices for *bias* and *focus*. Both *biassed* and *biased* and both *focussed* and *focused* are acceptable spellings.

> ***HINT*** Some spellings just have to be learned. Make a list of your own 'hard words'.

We spell words in English in the way we do for a variety of reasons, such as trying to represent:

- **a difference in meaning, despite a similarity in sound** – for example, *there, their, they're*;
- **related meanings, despite some variation in sound** – for example, *medicine, medical, medicinal*;
- **an earlier pronunciation** – for example, *knight*;
- **a foreign origin** – for example, *chalet.*

If the way we sound words was the only guide to their spelling, *phonics* might be spelled *fonnix*. Many English northerners say *look* to rhyme with *spook;* most southerners rhyme it with the northern *luck*. But the main reason for spelling words as we do is that they **represent the sounds we speak**. This often seems unlikely but it does account for more spelling features than any other factor. Therefore, it helps to use this when learning some words that are fairly regular phonically.

Some of the words that can be learned like this are:

homophone   *pronounce*   *pronunciation*   *effect*

It can help to see if a word you find hard to spell can be pronounced in a way that reminds you of its spelling. On the other hand, be careful. Some words have the same sound – in the following examples, *e* – but are written differently:

ate   *jeopardy*   *pleasure*   *said*

A few words are often pronounced wrongly. *Mischievous* is sometimes spoken with an *ee* sound before the *-ous* and the speller needs to beware of that influence.

Although the sound/letter correspondence is so important in English, it still needs to be recognised that there are many **homophones**: words that sound alike but do not look alike or mean the same thing.

Learn by heart words that cannot be learned in any other way. One other way, in some cases, might be to invent a mnemonic. The student who wrote:

The children took too my personality.

might have been helped by something like:

Two *days ago, I went* **to** *work despite feeling* **too** *tired to get up.*

Other homophones include:

allot/a lot	*meet/meat/mete*
aloud/allowed	*pare/pear/pair*
ate/eight	*practise/practice*
doe/dough	*read/red*
due/dew	*sore/saw*
hare/hair	*wait/weight*
lead/led	*wear/where*
lent/leant	*wheel/weal*

Incidentally, although students have asked on three occasions for an 'explanation of the difference between *as* with an *h* and *as* without an *h*', this is not strictly a homophone. It is simply a reminder that the way in which any of us speaks is not always a good guide to how words are written.

Some words seem to be easily confused. Students have written:

people off all ages

instead of:

people of all ages.

Some write:

could of

instead of:

could have.

The main reason for this error is that *could have* is often abbreviated in speech to *could've*. The pronunciation of *could've* is almost identical to that of *could of*, which is a spelling error. The pronunciation of *should've, must've, would've,* etc. (the abbreviations of *should have, must have, would have,* etc.) accounts for the frequent spelling confusions of *should of, must of, would of,* etc.

The difference is in meaning in the case of *off* instead of *of* and in grammar in the case of *of* instead of *have*. *Off* is used to mean something like *movement from a position*, as in *jump off, take off, off with his head*. After a modal verb such as *could*, you need another, main, verb such as *have*, not a preposition like *of*.

Some words are best learned by heart, such as either those that look as if, by analogy, they should be spelled like another word you know or those that simply have no analogy. These include such words as:

awe	*ladle*	*rhythm*
awful	*merit*	*sceptic*
curiosity	*mileage*	*schedule*
curious	*monotonous*	*scheme*
eighth	*naive*	*separate*
fifth	*occasion*	*sixth*
half	*prestige*	*suspicion*
halves	*prevail*	*table*
heroes	*prevalent*	*thorough*
humorous	*psychiatrist*	*tried*
humour	*pursue*	*try*
ideology	*queue*	*twelfth*
judgement	*repertoire*	*unanimous*
label	*rhyme*	*vicious*

Notice that some words have a pattern of letters that is fairly consistent – for example, the four-vowel pattern of a repeated *ue* in *queue*, the *-ous* ending in *humorous*. Some words, like *prevail* and *prevalent*, not only add a morpheme (such as *-ent*) when they become another part of speech but also change the spelling of the stem word (the *i* is dropped from *prevail* as the *u* is dropped from *humour* when it is changed to *humorous*).

Some words are spelled one way when they are nouns and another way when they are verbs:

Noun: *practice*   *advice*   Verb: *practise*   *advise*

If you could say *the* before a word, it is a noun and ends in *-ice*. If you could say *I*, *you*, *we*, *they* before it, it is a verb and ends in *-ise*.

Some long words can be broken down into parts:

miscellany = misc + ell + any

You need to notice the features of each part: the *sc*; the double *ll*; the recognisable word *any*.

Some words can be broken down into smaller words:

weather = w + eat + her   *together = to + get + her*

We confess our indebtedness to a boy aged five for revealing that truth about *together*!

Remember the patterns – the sequences of letters – in words that repeat particular letters:

minimise   *curriculum*   *remember*

Remember is often misspelled, simply because of the crowded repetition of *e* and *m*.

Notice what happens when a **suffix** is added.

Just as *humour* loses its second *u* when it becomes *humorous,* so we find other changes when a word takes a suffix:

To form the plural of a word that ends in *y*, drop the *y* and add *ies*:

fairy   fairies   country   countries

To add *-ed* or *-ing* to a verb that ends in *-e*, drop the *e*:

manage   managed   managing
create   created   creating
solve   solved   solving

To add *-ed* or *-ing* to a verb with a short vowel sound, double the final consonant:

rap   rapped

To add *-ed* or *-ing* to a verb with a long vowel sound, keep the final consonant single:

reap   reaped

If you can develop a feel for the ways that English words are built, for their **morphology**, it will help you to see where one part ends and another begins. This can help particularly with longer and less common words and with the common affixes:

mis + take   dis + tinc + tion   dis + agree + able

It is not obvious but the suffix is *-tion,* not *-ion.*

HINT   Note that the prefixes *mis* and *dis* end in one *s* only. That helps when you add *dis* to *appear* to make *disappear*: not *dissappear.*

Some words, connected by meaning – and in these cases, therefore, by spelling – vary a little in the way they sound but that has to be ignored:

photo   photograph   photographer   photographic

The letters *sc* represent the *s* sound if the following letter is *e* or *i*:

discipline   adolescent   descent

On the other hand, they represent the *sk* sound if the following letter is *r, l, a, o, u*:

discrepancy   discussion

When do you write *ie* and when do you write *ei*? This rule works:

For the sound *ee*, put *ie* as in:

  believe *mischief* *niece*

For the sound *ee*, put *e* before *i* when the preceding letter is *c*:

  conceive *deceive* *receive*

However, this only applies to words where the sound is *ee* and not to words like:

  weight *forfeit* *friend*

Many people ignore that last part of the rule.

> **HINT** *i* before *e*, except after *c*, when the sound is *ee*.

Most words that end with the sound in *rec**ent*** use *-ent*:

confident	*emergent*	*equivalent*	*excellent*
impatient	*independent*	*prevalent*	*reminiscent*

Very few words use *-ant*:

  preponderant *quadrant* *redundant*

> **HINT** Since far more words end in *-ent or -ence*, it pays to focus on and learn any that end in *-ant* or *-ance*.

A very common error is to use the wrong letters to represent the vowel sound in *sir*. Words like these just have to be learned by heart:

  *p**ur**sue* *sep**ar**ate* *b**ir**d* *w**or**d*

The sound *s* is often written with a *c*, especially if the *c* is followed by an *e* or *i*, as in:

  concede *deficit* *necessary*

Sometimes, it is written with a *-ce*, especially at the end of a word:

  practice *prejudice*

Sometimes, it is written with an *s*, even when it is not expected:

  idiosyncrasy *consensus* *supersede*

Or with an *-se*:

practise   *premise*

And even with *-sc*:

miscellaneous   *miscellany*   *scene*

General tips

Keep a dictionary nearby to check problem words and then try to learn them. Look out for commonly used letter-strings, for affixes and other morphological features and simply for anything unusual.

See if you tend to make particular errors, such as not noticing that *separate* has an *a* in the middle or that *develop*, unlike *envelope*, does not end with an *e*.

Try sounding out. On the whole, words that are phonically regular do not cause spelling problems but some writers lose their faith in that regularity. Try it.

Look at the whole of a word, not just its individual letters, and try to remember that whole. If it helps, say the letters to yourself rhythmically.

Look for possible analogies, for example, *eight*, *height* and *weight*.

Pay special attention to the letter-strings in foreign words. Their foreignness includes their combining letters differently from English:

fjord   craic   khaki   macho   graffiti   Pilsner   cha siu

Do not trust the spell check on a word processor. Any spell check will allow *top* when you meant *to*, *were* when you meant *where* and *feather* when you meant *father*. A spell check will correct non-words, like *teh* when the writer intended *the*, but it is still necessary to read through a late draft to check the spelling yourself.

If you know which words you tend to get wrong when you use a word processor *(have* and *because*, in my case!), go to *Tools, Autocorrect* and type in both the way you regularly type them (wrongly) and also the correct way. The processor will then automatically correct your spelling. But remember that this does nothing for your own ability to spell!

Questions

In the Literacy Skills Test you will be asked to spell ten words. These will be examples of words that are most likely to be encountered within the professional context of teaching. They represent the vocabulary, and its correct spelling, that fellow professionals, parents and pupils would expect every teacher to know.

All the words below are in general use; some follow generic spelling rules and some are spellings that just have to be learned by heart.

Select the correctly spelled word from the box of alternatives. Write your answer in the space in the sentence.

Questions

1. Annie enjoyed doing so much _____ work on her Charlemagne Extended Project Qualification.

indipendent
indipendant
independent
independant

2. The group had made _____ progress with their task.

demonstrible
demonstratable
demonstrable
demonstreble

3. Some useful _____ resources can be found on the internet.

asessment
assessmant
assesment
assessment

4. Research shows there is a marked increase in creativity during _____.

adolescence
adolescents
adolesence
adolesensce

5. Pupils were encouraged to _____ their own reading topics.

persue
purrsue
parsue
pursue

6. Most of the class found the _____ in the school's production of *A Midsummer Night's Dream* quite unconvincing.

fairys
faries
fairies
fareys

Questions

7. _____ ingredients in Home Economics assessed the pupils' numeracy skills.

Weighting
Wieghing
Weighing
Waying

8. The prospect of visiting the coast _____ the pupils' enthusiasm for the project.

fuelled
feulled
fueled
fuled

9. Some of the pupils were deeply _____ by the contents of the diaries.

effected
afected
efected
affected

10. Two posts offering greater _____ were being advertised in the school.

responsability
responserbility
responsibility
responsebilty

11. Most pupils found the _____ tests very helpful.

practise
practiss
practisce
practice

12. The experiment proved that substances do not _____ when they dissolve.

disapear
dissappear
disappear
disappeare

Questions

13. Field trip regulations include strict regulations about the _____ of knives.

possession
posession
possesion
possessions

14. It proved _____ to move the whiteboard just for one meeting.

impracticible
unpracticible
impracticable
unpracticable

15. The class responded well to the range of _____ poems their teacher presented.

humouros
humorous
humourous
hummorous

16. The small sample shows how percentages can give an _____ impression.

exagerated
exaggarated
exagarated
exaggerated

17. _____ the heavy snow meant that the school concert had to be postponed.

Regretably
Regrettably
Regrettebly
Regreatably

18. Some left-handed pupils _____ write across the page from right to left.

automaticly
autimatically
automaticaly
automatically

Questions

19. The conference addressed new approaches to _____ delivery.

    curiculum
    curriculum
    curicullum
    curicculum

20. Some pupils may not admit to problems with mathematics due to _____.

    embarassment
    embarrasment
    embarrassment
    embarasment

21. Teachers need a sound knowledge of their subject areas and related _____.

    pedergogy
    pedogogy
    pedagogy
    pedagogey

22. Pupils are _____ to attend school in casual clothing on Own Clothes Day.

    aloud
    allowed
    alowed
    aloued

23. When he came to _____ art materials among the children he was working with, Joe found that he had miscounted.

    alot
    a lot
    alott
    allot

24. The junior school choir sang with a _____ that was beyond their age.

    maturity
    maturaty
    matturity
    maturety

25. Support and _____ are key parts of the anti-bullying policy.

    counciling
    counselling
    counsiling
    councelling

26. What had once seemed a _____ collection of options now seemed very logical.

    miscellanious
    miscellaneous
    missellanious
    miscelanious

27. My answer to the question about death rates in Napoleon's army had to be an _____.

    aproximation
    approximation
    approximacion
    approcsimacion

28. It was clearly _____ of me to be late for the exam.

    reprehensable
    repprehensable
    repprehensabel
    reprehensible

29. Irina spent weeks discussing whether a degree or an _____ would suit her better.

    apprenticeship
    aprenticeship
    aprentiship
    aprentiseship

3.3 Punctuation

Introduction

15 marks are available for punctuation. That is almost halfway to the pass mark.

Punctuation has often been undervalued yet its importance in conveying your meaning to a reader clearly and unambiguously is great. Poor or missing punctuation can lead to the reader getting a quite false impression, as in:

> *After we left the pupils, the parents and I went to meet the headteacher.*

if what you meant was:

> *After we left, the pupils, the parents and I went to meet the headteacher.*

In the second sentence the comma changes the meaning so that it is clear that the pupils also went to meet the headteacher.

A literate teacher may need to check his or her spelling often but is, by definition, able to use punctuation well.

The aspects of punctuation in the test are concerned with ways in which writers mark off *units of meaning* (such as a sentence), ways in which the actual status of the language being used is clarified and ways in which words themselves are punctuated.

The main ways of marking 'units of meaning'

Any text is made up of parts: the whole text, the paragraphs, the sentences, the clauses and the phrases. These are the units of meaning greater than the individual word. The main ways in which we mark off where one unit ends and another begins are:

- paragraph;
- full stop;
- comma.

None of these is straightforward; all are partly a matter of personal style. Consequently, the key is to be consistent with punctuation within any one text.

Paragraphing

A paragraph is a group of one or more sentences that have enough related meaning, enough similarity in content or topic, to form a group. The writer decides where to begin and end each paragraph, depending on how he or she regards the main groups of meaning. A good text is divided along consistent lines, following the same idea about what makes a chunk of meaning, and one sentence within the paragraph states the main idea. This is the topic sentence; it often comes first.

Good paragraphing also makes considered use of sentence adverbs, those connectives, such as *However, Furthermore, On the other hand, Fortunately,* etc., that link the meaning of the new paragraph to the previous one.

However, the choice of where to start a new paragraph can sometimes be very subjective. The main reason is to show when a writer is:

- switching to a new idea;
- highlighting an important point;
- showing a change in time or place;
- emphasising a contrast; or
- indicating progression toward a summary or conclusion.

The test might show you a text that could have paragraphs but that is printed without any; you might be asked to identify where paragraph boundaries could come.

> **HINT** If you are uncertain about inserting a paragraph break, check the number of definite punctuation omissions you have already amended. Remember, there are only 15 unequivocally missing pieces of punctuation. If you have made 14 changes and cannot see another obvious omission, apart from the need for a paragraph break, this is probably the fifteenth instance where punctuation is needed.

Full stop

Full stops define a sentence, literally, by showing its limit. You need to develop a sense of what a sentence is to use full stops properly. If the largest unit of meaning is the unbroken, complete text and the next largest is the paragraph, the largest below that is the sentence. As a rule, it is one or more clauses long, has a sense of relative completeness about it and usually has a verb and its subject.

Over 80 per cent of all the punctuation marks used in British English are full stops and commas.

> **HINT** To help you to get a better grip of sentences and their need for a final full stop, look at *Clause, Sentence* and *Verb* in the Glossary. Keep that in mind as you read about commas.

Commas

It is not a simple task to use commas well. The first and simplest guidance is:

if you are not sure whether to use a comma or a full stop, use a full stop and begin a new sentence.

It was just what I had been looking for, from my experience with the previous class I felt a need for children who wanted to learn.

should be:

It was just what I had been looking for. From my experience with the previous class, I felt a need for children who wanted to learn.

Commas help us to separate items in a list. They can, therefore, be used as an alternative to the word *and* **but not as well as** *and*:

Above all, Zeinab likes to teach maths, geography, art and history.

You do not need a comma after *art* because *and* here does the job of a comma. This could be written using *and* instead of a comma:

Above all, Zeinab likes to teach maths and geography and art and history.

Sometimes, we use a phrase or word at the beginning of a sentence and then start to write what we mean.

The sentence above is an example: it begins with *sometimes* and then continues with the subject of the sentence, *we*. Put a comma after that opening word or phrase before continuing with what you want to say. Apart from that *sometimes*, other common **sentence-openers**, or sentence adverbs, are:

On the other hand,
However,
Suddenly,
Next,
Instead,
Unfortunately,

Sometimes, we want to vary what we say by changing the order in which we say things. This might be because we want to *emphasise* **something or other:**

My last tutor asked if he could copy my maths plans because he felt that they were a good model.

This could be turned round without changing, adding or omitting any words but by adding a comma at the break:

Because he felt that they were a good model, my last tutor asked if he could copy my maths plans.

This is a rather tricky use of the comma. It can be important because it tells the reader precisely what the meaning is. The use of commas can put an end to *ambiguity.* **This comma-free sentence is ambiguous:**

The teachers who live in Gotham are all over six feet tall.

As it stands, this seems *very* improbable. But suppose the sentence is just about a group of people over six feet who simply happen to live in Gotham. That is more than probable. The fact that they live in Gotham is almost an afterthought. The essence of the sentence, the main clause, is:

The teachers are all over six feet tall.

Now, an extra, incidental bit of information is given. It is a relative clause:

who live in Gotham

This extra clause can be **embedded** in (set inside) the main clause. To show that it is extra, it is separated from the rest by commas:

The teachers, who live in Gotham, are all over six feet tall.

(This use of the embedded clause is a sophistication that the devisers of the Primary National Strategy wanted to see promoted in schools.)

Not only clauses are embedded. We embed phrases and single words. They may appear at the beginning of a sentence (see the opening sentence adverbs above), in the middle or at the end. Children can be helped by having a discussion about what to embed in a sentence (if anything) and where in the sentence the embedded item might go:

Naturally, the choice of where to apply was rather limited.

or:

The choice of where to apply was rather limited, naturally.

or:

The choice of where to apply was, naturally, rather limited.

The embedded item is bounded by a capital letter and a comma at the beginning of the sentence, by a comma and a full stop at the end and by two, paired commas in the middle.

When we write *dialogue*, a comma ends the text before the quotation marks and the spoken words begin:

Gobinda said, 'Come along with me, children.'

What commas cannot do is end a sentence.

Additional ways of marking 'units of meaning'

These additional ways are the use of:

- colon;
- semicolon;
- question mark;
- brackets.

Colon
The commonest use of the colon is to introduce a list:

The children brought a wealth of evidence from the playground: sweet wrappers, milk straws, cards to swap, crisp packets and some cigarette packets.

Another use is to introduce some reasoning or evidence to support the part of the sentence that comes before the colon:

Some of them blamed the secondary school children: they reminded the class that several teenagers regularly took a short cut across their playground.

Semicolon

The semicolon is rarely used in the writing of many people; not only students and teachers but some of our greatest writers ignore this mark. It is possible to write without using it but it can allow a writer to put two independent clauses together that could stand as individual sentences but that the writer feels are unusually closely related. This book contains examples in its text.

Another use of the semicolon is to mark off items in a list following a colon, especially if the items in the list are each several words long:

The school still had some problems: a falling roll; two teachers due to retire within the year; an imminent Ofsted inspection.

However, commas can also do that job. Be careful: if one of those items has so many words that the phrase itself needs a comma, all the items must be separated by a semicolon.

Question mark

This mark ends a sentence that asks a question:

Is your personal statement nearly ready?

Will we need supply cover for next Tuesday?

It is not necessary at the end of a sentence that implies a question but that has the structure of a statement (that is, the subject comes before the verb):

I wonder if there will be any supply teachers available.

I asked him when he would be ready for swimming.

If the sentence is within quotation marks, the question mark comes before the final quotation mark:

'Can we get together about this Performance Management meeting?'

'Could you tell me why your assignment is 3,000 words over the limit?'

Brackets or parentheses

These marks (the two words really mean the same) begin and end an aside in a sentence. Often, a writer composes a sentence but wants to add something to it that is not strictly part of the sentence; rather, it is almost an afterthought or something that he or she would like to say as well as the sentence:

> *Not many of us (at least, not those under 60) can remember what it was like to teach in those controversial times.*

> *We have had no child statemented (none that we were successful in having statemented, anyway!) for over five years now.*

HINT Look at *Parenthesis* in the Glossary.

Punctuation which indicates the status of the language being used

The status of the language being used is shown by the use of:

- **speech marks;**
- **quotation marks.**

Speech marks (double quotes) and quotation marks (single quotes) can help you to make it clear to the reader that this or that piece of your writing is to be read in a particular way. Both can be, and are, in some published texts, used to mark **direct speech,** such as the dialogue in a story.

A teacher might write a story with a class. Any dialogue, words actually spoken by a character, will need to be put inside **speech marks:**

> *When Fergus the king asked Nes to be his wife, she replied, "Only if I get something in return."*

> *"What is that?" he asked.*

Quotation marks can be used for the same purpose but they are valuable in their own right. They can draw the reader's attention to the way that some word or phrase sits oddly in the text as a whole:

> *When buying travel insurance for their children, parents and carers are advised to be mindful of the so-called 'get out clause' used by some insurance firms.*

They help the reader to see that a part of the text actually comes from some source other than the writer:

Song asked his teacher for help with his exposé but was told to 'just get on with it'.

They tell the reader that some of the text is the name of a film or the title of a book:

Shamila started to read 'Harry Potter and the Goblet of Fire' but the spiders scared her so she stopped.

HINT Parentheses, speech marks and quotation marks all work in pairs. If the test shows just one parenthesis or speech/quotation mark, you know that there has to be another. Look for where it might be.

Punctuation within words

The marks that occur within single words are:

- hyphens;
- apostrophes;
- capital letters.

They give the reader information about that word, rather than showing how larger units of meaning are organised or bounded.

Hyphens

Hyphens link two words that have another meaning when they occur together. Some of the first elements are words in themselves, others are abbreviations or suffixes:

well-stocked, ex-headteacher, post-Ofsted, pro-uniform, U-turn, T-shirt

This sort of hyphenated word is a kind of halfway point between two words and one.

Apostrophes

The apostrophe, a minefield for some writers, has two main uses but is sometimes wrongly used for a third purpose.

Abbreviation or omission

When we write, we sometimes choose to leave letters out of words to get closer to the way we speak English. Because we rarely sound the full value of *we will, we do not, we shall not, we cannot*, we may abbreviate them:

we'll, don't, shan't, can't

One of the trickiest of these abbreviations is the use of *it's*, easily confused with *its*. The solution is simply never to write *it's*. *It's* is always an abbreviation, usually of *it is* but sometimes of *it has*. Abbreviations are normal in informal writing but unknown in formal texts. Only use *it's* when you mean to write an informal text and when you mean either *it is* or *it has*:

It's appropriate to write formally.

means the same as:

It is appropriate to write formally.

It's become obvious that clear writing matters.

means the same as:

It has become obvious that clear writing matters.

You will then write *its* only without an apostrophe and only when it is appropriate: as the direct equivalent of *her* or *his* before a noun:

The new teaching assistant put down her bag, helped Nathan out of his wheelchair and covered its seat with a cushion.

Only use the apostrophe as abbreviation when you feel quite confident and in control as a writer.

HINT Never write *it's*. Write *it is* or *it has* instead and you can forget that apostrophe problem.

Possession

Books have titles. Write down who or what *possesses* the titles:

the book

then put an apostrophe:

the book'

and ask: does this word end with the letter *s*? If not, add one:

the book's

and continue:

the book's title.

If there are several books, you would have the sequence:

the books

then put an apostrophe

the books'

and ask: does this word end with the letter *s*? If it does, leave it alone:

the books'

and continue:

the books' titles.

There is no need to think about singular or plural provided you place the apostrophe before you check if the word ends in *s* or not. Of course, the way this works means that, in most cases, the placing of the apostrophe does say whether the word before is singular or plural but that does not always help. If men have ambitions and you want to write about that affliction, the singular and plural – *man* and *men* – would look like this:

the man	*the men*
the man'	*the men'*
the man's	*the men's*
the man's ambitions	*the men's ambitions*

The wrong use of the apostrophe plus *s* as a plural form
The sight of cards on market stalls saying *Cabbage's* and *Cauliflower's* (and *Ca'fe* in one town) has led to the rather unfair name of *Greengrocers' Apostrophe* for this wrong use of *'s* instead of the simple plural 's'.

There is a special, and wrong, case of the apostrophe-as-plural that goes far beyond the efforts of any greengrocer. We now have quite a few words in English that end with a vowel, especially *o*: *video, studio, radio, data, scampi, criteria,* etc. Some people add *'s* to these words to indicate a plural: *video's,* etc. There is no need. For most of these words, simply add *s* (the commonest way of making plurals in English). In the case of *data* and *media* and *criteria*, these words are already plural; there is no need to add anything to them at all. However, you can only have one criterion and many criteria and one medium being part of the media.

Capital letters
A capital letter is always needed at the beginning of a new sentence:

Only in my wildest dreams could I have succeeded in obtaining a place on such a course.

It is needed for titles and proper nouns: the names of people and places:

The letter from the Headteacher, Mrs Pendlebury, welcomed me to Ordsall.

There is no need to use a capital for *headteacher* if there is no name to follow.

Questions

Like all the tests, this one is computerised. Details of what you do in the test and how you do it are on page 26, but it will also help you a lot to look at the website http://media.education.gov.uk/assets/files/pdf/l/literacy%20skills%20test%20 specification.pdf. If you want to change anything, that can be done. You will not need to delete any punctuation.

The test will present you with a text from which much of the punctuation has been deleted. Your task is to create a properly punctuated complete text from this incomplete one. The key thing, again, is consistency: read the text and its existing punctuation as information about how to complete it. Remember, there are only 15 omissions of punctuation in the test.

The passages below are examples of the kind of test you will have.

Since you are doing this test in a book and not on a computer, read the whole passage and add any punctuation you feel is necessary in pencil or by making a note. Where you want to change a lower case to a capital letter, put a circle round the letter and write *cap* in the margin; where you want a new paragraph, put a forward slash (/) immediately before the first word of the new paragraph and write *np* in the margin.

1. As soon as we speak we reveal a great deal of ourselves to our audience. Suppose you ask someone,

    "shall we have a drink

    Suppose the other person replies

    "Yes, I'd like a whiskey me."

    That tag, *me*, tells you that the speaker probably comes from manchester.

    Sometimes, what people say does tell you something about their origin but it is less definite. A friend asks you and another friend,

    "Now, what would youse two like to drink?"

    The questioner may or may not come from Ireland but will certainly have a background there because that use of youse, unknown in Standard English, has its roots in the Irish having one form of 'you' for one person tú and another form of 'you' for two people sibh. However none of this means that any of these speakers could actually speak any Irish!

2. The concern of the head of english was evident after reading the 'Can do Better' report on literacy. If we look at boys performance in English, we have to agree that there is, generally some cause for concern. Is there anything that can be done to help them improve?

Questions

Among the short term approaches that seemed to help boys are enthusiastically encouraged private reading;

clearly set tasks

explicit teaching of reading strategies;

a wide range of outcomes from reading;

reading preferences that are discussed.

3. What is it about Standard English that makes it standard Like every language, English has gone through many changes. The Saxons and Angles who settled here brought their own languages with them predominantly Saxon, and after a while the dialects of Anglo-Saxon overcame the Celtic languages that had flourished along with Latin until soon after the Romans left in 410 AD. The languages spoken by the later Scandinavian invaders were probably just about intelligible to some of the Anglo Saxons but changes and borrowings continued: the new invaders legacy to us includes **they, them, their**. Anglo-Saxon, modified by Scandinavian, with dialects that were barely intelligible to other Anglo-Saxon speakers, continued for hundreds of years but, thankfully it became simpler The German word for **big** is **gross** but it has six versions. Our Anglo-Saxon ancestors had eleven versions of adjectives we have just three: **big, bigger, biggest**. Even when we complicate matters by having **good, better best**, that is still easier than Anglo-Saxon.

3.4 Grammar

Introduction

8–12 marks are available for grammar.

One of the main jobs of a teacher is to work with colleagues in producing documents for a variety of audiences, from known people within the school to outside bodies, and for a range of purposes, from planning teaching to explaining and presenting work that has been done. That collaboration involves drafting, redrafting and proof-reading. This test does not test your writing nor your knowledge of grammatical terms; rather, it will test:

- **your grasp of written Standard English;**
- **your ability to identify and use it unambiguously;**
- **your understanding of which style is appropriate to the text in question.**

How will these three aspects of grammatical knowledge be tested? What, in detail, do those aspects mean you need to know?

The grammar section of the test presents you with two or three short pieces of text. The text is usually an example of the everyday reading or writing material that a teacher might be expected to encounter in the course of their professional duties. Such texts might include:

- notes or letters to parents and carers;
- notes or letters to or from colleagues;
- minutes of meetings;
- information about training and professional development;
- articles for school newsletters or websites.

Within the document there are gaps in the text. At these points there is a question with multiple choices. Four options are provided as possible alternatives to fill the gap; only one is correct. The three remaining distracters contain faults and are incorrect. People who already use English competently and with confidence would not make such faults and would notice them in the writing of other people or, perhaps, in an early draft of their own work.

The items of grammatical knowledge that will be tested are set out and explained below.

Consistency with written Standard English

Each test presents you with some examples of English; only one example is acceptable as Standard English. You have to choose and identify that one. To be able to do that, you need to have an awareness of what kinds of error are possible, of the features of non-Standard English and of the appropriate, standard alternative.

Here are the 24 Grammar issues <u>you must understand</u> before you sit the computerised Test. At least one question from each section will appear in the computerised test.	
1.	**Consistency with written Standard English**
1	Sentence boundaries
2	Faulty sentence construction
3	Lack of cohesion
4	Subject /verb agreement
5	Should have/of confusion etc.
6	Incomplete/inappropriate verbs
7	Prepositions
8	Noun pronoun agreement
9	Determiner/noun errors
10	Wrong/missing determiner
11	Comparatives/superlatives
12	Relative pronouns, subordinate clauses
13	Adverbial forms

(Continued)

(Continued)

2.	Sense clarity and freedom from ambiguity
14	Lack of coherence
15	Wrong tense inconsistency
16	Unrelated participles
17	Attachment ambiguities
18	Ambiguous pronoun references
19	Word confusion, imply /infer etc
3.	Professional suitability and style
20	Non parallelism in lists
21	Inconsistent register and tone
22	Shift in person
23	Redundancy/tautology
24	Inappropriate conjunctions

Failure to observe sentence boundaries

Perhaps the commonest failing in adults' writing is this problem with deciding where a sentence ends and needs a full stop (see section on punctuation). Be very wary of sentences that go on and on. It is very easy to ignore that length and, worse still, the complexity that falls into the sentence as it develops. It is far better to write more sentences, varying in complexity, with some short, simple, one-clause sentences among them. For example:

> *It was my great opportunity, from my experience with the previous class I knew how to make the most of the first group's ideas.*

should be:

> *It was my great opportunity. From my experience with the previous class, I knew how to make the most of the first group's ideas.*

Look at 'Comma' in the section on punctuation. Generally, unless you know you can write well, do not be too ambitious as a stylist. Your writing is more likely to be sound Standard English if you follow the advice about short sentences. If you are not sure whether it should be a comma or a full stop, put a full stop. In most cases, you will be safe.

> **HINT**   Use full stops more often.

Abandoned or faulty constructions and sentence fragments

A sentence should use consistent structures. It is very easy, especially if you write slowly, to lose track of the way you are writing, the structures you are using. The best way to avoid this problem is to reread what you write as you write and, particularly, to look out for any faults that you know you are prone to. Usually, the way that you begin the sentence is the way it should continue.

This is a faulty construction:

Concerned about the falling numbers in the city's schools so the Director of Education proposed that two primary schools should be closed and one re-opened as a junior school.

It should be either:

Concerned about the falling numbers in the city's schools, the Director of Education proposed that two primary schools should be closed and one re-opened as a junior school.

or:

The Director of Education proposed that two primary schools should be closed and one re-opened as a junior school because he was concerned about the falling numbers in the city's schools.

or:

Because he was concerned about the falling numbers in the city's schools, the Director of Education proposed that two primary schools should be closed and one re-opened as a junior school.

This is a sentence fragment:

Although there was still uncertainty about the best choice of software.

This has obviously become separated from the sentence of which it should be a part. In a sense, this is the other side of the previous problem with sentence boundaries: this time, the writer has probably put in an unnecessary full stop that cuts this fragment off from the rest. The whole sentence might have looked like this:

Although there was still uncertainty about the best choice of software, the Governors decided to go ahead with the purchase of new computers.

Here, the full sentence is given and the whole is much easier to grasp. The word 'sentence' is notoriously difficult to define but those criteria of completeness and comprehensibility are central.

An alternative to that whole sentence would be:

The Governors decided to go ahead with the purchase of new computers although there was still uncertainty about the best choice of software.

It is worth noting here, as in some other examples in this book, that there are often at least two ways to structure a sentence, often with little or no change to the words themselves. What has been altered here in the two acceptable alternatives is the sequence of the two clauses and the punctuation: if the minor (subordinate or dependent) clause comes first, separate it from the following main clause with a comma.

> **HINT**   Get into the habit, when you read a text, of seeing if some of its sentences can be restructured.

Lack of cohesion

Most of us think of grammar as the way that words are combined to make phrases, clauses and sentences. In recent decades, a lot of attention has been paid to the way that sentences are also linked together so that we know that this series of sentences is one text, not a random collection from different texts. All of us automatically use a variety of ways to make our writing (and our speech) link together as a whole, to give it cohesion.

Lack of cohesion is what happens when the writer has not made the links between sentences – or within them – as clear as they would be if they were cohesive. Cohesion deals with the various ways in which writers create these clear links. The test focuses on one of these ways, the cohesive link that depends on the appropriate use of pronouns (see the section on punctuation, and *Cohesion*, *Connective* and *Pronoun* in the Glossary).

This short passage lacks cohesion:

> *A first-year **student** should receive good support from the tutors and from the student union. Nevertheless, **they** have substantial responsibility.*

What is wrong here is that the noun *student* is singular but the pronoun that refers to it, *they*, is plural. This is a common error and can only be rectified by rereading as you write, checking each use of a pronoun and making sure that there is no ambiguity about which noun it refers to.

The two sentences above should read:

> *First-year **students** should receive good support from the tutors and from the student union. Nevertheless, **they** have substantial responsibility.*

Here, both the noun and its pronoun are plural. Sometimes the pronoun needs to be changed and sometimes, as here, it is easier to change the noun. It would be possible to revise the two problem sentences like this:

*A first-year **student** should receive good support from the tutors and from the student union but would, nevertheless, have substantial responsibility.*

Here, there would be a problem in choosing a pronoun because English has only *he* or *she*, neither of which is acceptable here. One way to get round this little problem is to leave out the pronoun altogether, as the sentence above shows. That omission of a word that would normally be present is another kind of **cohesive device**: ellipsis.

Lack of agreement between subject and verb

This is another very common error. It can show itself in many ways:

- two nouns (e.g. *maths and English*) with a singular verb (e.g. *is*);
- plural determiner (e.g. *these*) with a singular verb (e.g. *was*);
- singular determiner (e.g. *this*) with a plural verb (e.g. *were*);
- singular verb (e.g. *is*) with some non-English plurals (e.g. *data*).

Here are some examples of those four basic kinds of error.

Two nouns with a singular verb:

*Underlying the good SAT results **was** the hard **work** of the pupils and a determined **staff.***

This should be:

*Underlying the good SAT results **were** the hard **work** of the pupils and a determined **staff.***

The subject of the verb *was* is plural: *work* and *staff*; two nouns make a plural subject. If the subject is plural, the verb should be plural: *were*.

Plural determiner with a singular verb:

***Some** teachers who had been trained in ICT **has** made excellent use of word processing.*

Some is a plural determiner – it introduces a plural noun, *teachers* – so it needs a plural verb: *have*, not *has*. That sentence should read:

***Some** teachers who had been trained in ICT **have** made excellent use of word processing.*

Singular determiner with a plural verb:

*Many of us grew up with a very prescriptive view of language without realising that **that** view of grammar **were** inadequate.*

The second use of *that* is a singular determiner so it needs a singular verb: *was*, not *were*.

That sentence should read:

> *Many of us grew up with a very prescriptive view of language without realising that* **that** *view of grammar* **was** *inadequate.*

As you probably noticed, most of these determiners can also function as pronouns.

Singular verb with some non-English plurals:

> *There was some argument about the findings because the research* **criteria was** *in dispute.*

The word *criteria* is a plural because it comes from Greek and follows a Greek way of forming plurals. The singular form is *criterion*. Since *criteria* is plural, the verb should be *were*:

> *There was some argument about the findings because the research* **criteria were** *in dispute.*

An equally safe version would be:

> *There was some argument about the findings because the research* **criterion was** *in dispute.*

Of course, the meanings of the two sentences would be different!

English uses many words that still have their original forms of singular and plural. Some people feel that, when they are used in English, those singular and plural forms should still be used. At the moment, for instance, it seems that there is still a useful distinction in English between *criterion* and *criteria* that is worth retaining. On the other hand, some foreign loan-words are known in English in either, predominantly, a plural form (for example, *graffiti*, *agenda*, *data*) or a singular form (for example, *rhododendron*). Few of us talk of *graffito* or *rhododendra* for the simple reason that we do not know the Italian or Greek plurals (and, if we did, who – or whom – would we talk to?).

All language changes and that applies to Standard English as well as to other varieties. It is likely that words like *data* will settle down as singular forms because nobody else uses them as plural. Perhaps *data* itself will become both singular and plural, rather like *sheep*. *Criterion* and *criteria* are easier words to use confidently because both are used quite widely in British English. The point about using Standard English is to use the variety of it that is being used and understood currently.

This degree of uncertainty also applies to some other parts of this book. You will find at least as much uncertainty about these and other matters in Bill Bryson's helpful book, *Troublesome Words*.

Of all the words that still use their original, foreign plural forms, *data* and *criteria* are probably the ones most likely to be used by people in education.

Should have/of, might have/of

English makes a lot of use of modal verbs like *would*, *could*, *must*, *need not* and *ought to*, followed by the verb *have*. When we speak, we usually abbreviate *have* to a sound that we write as *'ve*. So we write *might have*, *should have*, etc. The pronunciation of *could've* is almost identical to that of *could of*, which is an error. The pronunciation of *should've*, *must've*, *would've*, etc. (the abbreviations of *should have*, *must have*, *would have*, etc.) accounts for the frequent confusions of *should of*, *must of*, *would of*, etc. It is always wrong to write *of* in these constructions. It is always right to write *have*.

> *In the headteacher's view, the school might not **of** been put under Special Measures if the stable staffing the school had benefited from earlier had been maintained.*

This should read:

> *In the headteacher's view, the school might not **have** been put under Special Measures if the stable staffing the school had benefited from earlier had been maintained.*

It is always worth bearing in mind that written Standard English is different from any spoken English in many ways and that it is not safe to rely too much on the sounds that are spoken as a guide to the way that the words are written. Nobody pronounces the last letter in *comb* but most of us put it in when we write the word.

Inappropriate or incomplete verb forms

One recommendation that is made repeatedly in this book is to reread what you write as you write. Even good writers can make embarrassing mistakes if they do not check what they write (this is being written by someone who consistently typed *the* as *teh* until he persuaded the Tools/Autocorrect facility to sort it out automatically). Whole words can be missed out, especially if the writer's attention is focused on another bit of the content. You need to be aware of this tendency that we all have and to pay particular attention to a fairly common error: the verb form that is either not appropriate or that is missing altogether.

> *Most of the class had learned use the spell check by half-term.*

This should read:

> *Most of the class had learned **to** use the spell check by half-term.*

One possible factor affecting this problem is that there are constructions in American English that do omit the word *to*: for example, *That afternoon, the class decided to **go explore** the neighbouring building site.* In British English, the word *to* would be used: *That afternoon, the class decided to **go to explore** the neighbouring building site.* The test is based on British English.

Sometimes, the verb itself gets left out:

Later, most of the children to show their findings to the headteacher.

This should read:

*Later, most of the children **wanted** to show their findings to the headteacher.*

It should be obvious that *wanted* is not the only verb that could fit this space but some verb, in an appropriate tense, is certainly needed.

> **HINT** This is one area where, as a writer, you can rely on the way you use language when speaking.

Wrong or missing preposition, e.g. different from/than/to

Words like *with, near, to, towards, through, in, by,* etc. are prepositions. They are usually found between two nouns (*a cat **on** a mat*), a verb and a noun (*a cat sat **on** a mat*) or some other part of speech and a noun or pronoun (*older **than**.*) Despite what was said above, there are some bits of language that change very slowly, if at all, and prepositions are among them. We still use the same prepositions that our ancestors used centuries ago. Prepositions are a *closed* word class.

The problem with them – and it is a problem; adult users of English probably have more trouble with prepositions than with any other part of speech – is that it is very easy to use an inappropriate one. This can alter what we are trying to say and cause misunderstanding.

There are some prepositions that use more than one word: complex prepositions, such as *different from.* An alternative to this is *different to.* At the moment, the complex preposition *different than* is considered to be non-Standard English. In that case, do not use it in formal writing; that is, in most writing.

The performance of this year's Y2 class was quite different than last year's.

should be either:

The performance of this year's Y2 class was quite different from last year's.

or:

The performance of this year's Y2 class was quite different to last year's.

Noun/pronoun agreement error

If you substitute pronouns for nouns in these sentences, you will notice a change in the pronouns but not in the nouns:

The man liked the woman.

becomes:

He liked her.

The woman liked the man.

becomes:

She liked him.

Two nouns have become four pronouns.

Aloysius assaulted the entire staff of the school.

becomes:

He assaulted them.

The entire staff of the school wanted to exclude Aloysius.

becomes:

They wanted to exclude him.

Man, woman, Aloysius, entire staff of the school all remained the same wherever they were in the sentences and whatever job they were doing. Nouns do not change according to position and job (although they can take a plural *s/es* and a possessive *'s* or *s'*). On the other hand, pronouns change a lot:

I	*me*	*my*	*mine*	*myself*
you	*you*	*your*	*yours*	*yourself*
she	*her*	*her*	*hers*	*herself*
he	*him*	*his*	*his*	*himself*
it	*it*	*its*	*its*	*itself*
we	*us*	*our*	*ours*	*ourselves*
they	*them*	*their*	*theirs*	*themselves*

Some years ago, the Prime Minister of the day rejected criticisms 'about Mr Lamont and I'. That is a very common error that is easy to avoid if you ask yourself what you would put if Mr Lamont were not involved. Would you write or say:

about I

or would you say:

about me

The basic rule is to ignore the use of the pronouns (whether *he and I* or *her and me* or whichever) and to ask yourself: 'Would I use *I* here or would I use *me*?' So, just as you would almost certainly write:

I have an interview in Wythenshawe next week.

You should also write:

My friend and I have interviews in Wythenshawe next week.

As you would almost certainly write:

The head showed me round the school.

You should also write:

The head showed my friend and me round the school.

To write:

The head showed my friend and I round the school.

is an unusual example of non-standard Standard English, unusual because it is not the English of working-class users but that spoken by middle- or aspiring middle-class users of English who believe that the *he and I* form seems more acceptable. It isn't.

Try to remember a simple sentence, such as:

I love my mother.

The word *I* comes before the verb *love* and, because it comes before the verb in this very simple sentence, it is the subject of the verb and of the sentence. If you write:

My mother loves me.

the subject is *My mother*. You do not do the loving, you *are* the loved. You are the object of the verb and of the sentence. *I* is different from *me* because it has a different meaning and does a different job.

Determiner/noun agreement error
In a radio broadcast some years ago, the then Secretary of State for Education referred to:

Those sort of programmes.

This is the error that happens when you get confused about how to link a determiner – words like *all, some, three, many, that, those, my, the, a/an* – to its noun. Such errors happen most often in brief phrases followed by a verb. This sentence-opening is acceptable English:

Determiner	noun phrase	verb ...
This	*type of error*	*is ...*

It is acceptable because the determiner and the verb are singular and so is the *headword* of the noun phrase, *type*. You need to know which word in the phrase is the headword, the real centre of the phrase. If the headword is singular, the verb and the determiner should also be singular. If the headword is plural, the verb and the determiner should also be plural. It is common to find sentences like this:

Although drafting and redrafting have been requirements since the 1989 National Curriculum in English, these kinds of activity is stumbling blocks for many children.

This should be:

Although drafting and redrafting have been requirements since the 1989 National Curriculum in English, these kinds of activity are stumbling blocks for many children.

This error, which is far more widespread in speech, is easy to understand but it is still not acceptable as Standard English. The writer has been trapped into using the singular verb *is* because the nearest word that *looks* like a subject – but is not – is the singular noun *activity*. In noun-phrases like:

sorts of book

kinds of poetry

types of text

the headword in every case is a plural: *sorts*, *kinds*, *types*. That plural headword is followed by a preposition and a singular noun. The next word is likely to be a verb and, in Standard English, the verb has to agree with the headword of the noun phrase; that is, if the headword is plural, the verb should be plural, too.

So should the determiner.

Inappropriate or missing determiner

The singular determiners *this*, *that* and the plural determiners *these*, *those* are also called demonstrative pronouns. We said earlier that many determiners also act as pronouns.

If you were writing about your plans for the next half-term, you might begin:

*Mike needed to make sure that **the** key points made at **the** university Open Day were reflected in his personal statement.*

You would not – and should not – begin:

*Mike needed to make sure that **those** key points made at **that** university Open Day were reflected in his personal statement.*

What is wrong about the second usage is that the determiners *those* and *that* refer back to something that has already been said and this is the opening so nothing has been said. *The* is wholly appropriate in this case because it introduces and establishes what you are going to write about.

Problems with comparatives and superlatives

The computer that this is being written on is new but it is not as new as the one my friend recently bought. His computer is *newer*. He says that his son, being something of an expert in these matters, has just bought a computer that is so new that nothing newer exists! That computer is – for the moment – the newest.

We are all used to making comparisons between things and people. In Standard English, this is done by using one of the two comparative forms: add *-er* to an adjective, as happened with *new/newer*, or precede it with *more*, as with *more recent*. If we want to state the ultimate in such a series, it is superlative: superlatives are expressed by adding *-est*, as with *newest*, or by preceding the adjective with *most*, as in *most recent*.

In most cases, it makes sense to write sentences that contain comparatives or superlatives but not both.

> *If children are put into groups according to whatever seating arrangements suit the activity best, the result seems to be a class that is **calmest** and **more attentive**.*

This should be:

> *If children are put into groups according to whatever seating arrangements suit the activity best, the result seems to be a class that is **calmer** and **more attentive**.*

It is hard to imagine a situation where it would be appropriate to write *calmer and most attentive*. To avoid this, simply reread it yourself and ask if it feels as though it makes good sense.

Since the comparison between the computers mentioned earlier obviously depended on there being another computer to compare with the first, it was necessary to bring in a third computer to see which was the newest. Superlatives are used when three or more things are being compared and comparatives when two only are being compared. Yet it is common to write or say sentences like:

> *Pawel is the **tallest** twin.*

This should be:

> *Pawel is the **taller** twin.*

There are only two twins so a comparative form of *tall* is all that is needed.

> **HINT** Alice is tall; Lucy is the taller of the *two*; Annie and Joe are the smallest of the four cousins. Compare two, it's *taller*; compare three or more, one will be *tallest*.

Problems with relative pronouns in subordinate clauses

First, we will look at **subordinate clauses**.

Suppose you write a simple sentence, with one clause, a main clause; something like this:

I still need some information about my new class.

You can say something more, perhaps about why you need that information; something like this:

I still need some information about my new class so that I can plan to help them.

What you have added to that main clause is another one, subordinate to it, that is called, reasonably enough, a subordinate clause. It needs the main clause to make full sense. It is a clause because it has a verb – *can plan* – and a subject – *I*.

Next, look at **relative pronouns**. These are pronouns that can introduce a subordinate clause. Most subordinate clauses are introduced by connectives such as *and*, *so that*, *because*, *if*, *unless*, *although*. Some, however, are introduced by a pronoun. These relative pronouns refer back to a noun in the main clause. The relative pronouns are:

who, whom, which, that

They appear in sentences like these:

*The headteacher believed that the school needed a teacher **who** could develop ICT work.*

*After a lot of discussion, the interviewing panel agreed to appoint the candidate **whom** the headteacher preferred.*

*The Chair of the interviewing panel restated the criteria **which** they had drawn up.*

*The result of the interviews was one **that** the whole panel was happy with.*

It is also possible to leave out the relative pronoun in many cases. This sentence:

*She was the one **whom** they wanted.*

could also be written as:

*She was the one **that** they wanted.*

but also as:

She was the one they wanted.

The likely error that some fall into is to use a relative pronoun that is not appropriate. **Which** is the pronoun we use when we are dealing with inanimate things. It is appropriate in this sentence:

*Over the term, the class had read texts **which** really extended their range of interests and abilities.*

It is not appropriate in this sentence because teachers are not inanimate:

*They had chosen the teacher **which** the headteacher wanted.*

That should be either:

*They had chosen the teacher **whom** the headteacher wanted.*

or:

They had chosen the teacher the headteacher wanted.

When do you use **who** and when do you use **whom**? Whether you should use **who** or **whom** is the same question as whether to use **he** or **him**, **she** or **her**, **I** or **me**, **we** or **us**. Suppose you are writing a very formal piece and you try the two options in this sentence:

*The panel chose the candidate **who/whom** was best.*

Ask yourself whether you would be more likely to write:

She was best.

or:

Her was best.

Unless you have a very unusual and inadequate grasp of English, you would say *She was best*. That means you would choose *who*. On the other hand, if you wanted to write this sentence:

*The headteacher asked the rest of the panel **who/whom** they liked.*

You could ask yourself whether it would make more sense to write:

They liked she.

or:

They liked her.

You would choose *her* and so you would also choose *whom*.

Although many of us hardly ever use *whom*, especially when speaking, the test is based on formal writing and does expect it to be used.

Inappropriate or missing adverbial forms
Sometimes, we can confuse the use of an adjective and an adverb. We know that we can write:

Mushraf was a fast runner.

where *fast* is an adjective, rather like *quick*. However, we can also write:

Mushraf ran fast.

where *fast* is an adverb, just like *quickly*. We know that many adverbs do not end in *-ly*. This very reliable bit of knowledge might tempt some of us to write sentences like this, where an adjective is used instead of an adverb:

On the whole, student options were intelligent chosen.

This should be:

On the whole, student options were intelligently chosen.

This is not the sort of error that native users of a language tend to make but it is the sort that can easily creep into a written text. That is why we repeatedly advise you to read and reread as you write. Get a feel for the sense and the flow of what you write and for the tone of voice you are using as a writer.

Sense, clarity and freedom from ambiguity

Some fiction and much poetry deliberately make very profitable use of the ambiguities and optional meanings that can be made from language. Most writing, however, has to make clarity a priority. Make your writing as easy to read as possible; change anything that is ambiguous; check it all the time to make sure that it makes sense.

You will be tested on your ability to spot when a piece of writing is clear and when it is not. This means that you need to have a good idea of the part that grammar can play in helping a text to be clear. The test will show you examples of writing and ask you to identify which of several options would make the piece clear.

These are some of the factors that make writing unclear:

Lack of coherence
Some texts are easier to read than others. If it is easy to understand, it must be coherent: it has *coherence*; the bits hold together to make a whole. Writers use a variety of ways to make this happen; for example, that pronoun *this* refers back to the idea of coherence in the previous sentence. Pronouns are crucial in making links *between* sentences in a continuous text.

Writers use other devices to make clauses hold together *within* a sentence. For example, they use *connectives* so that one clause can be linked in meaning to another; in this sentence, *so that* is a connective, linking the main clause *they use connectives* to its subordinate clause.

That use of grammatical devices to create that coherence is called *cohesion*. Those devices are called *cohesive devices*. There are several others that are not discussed here.

In the test, you will be asked to identify when a text lacks coherence because there are problems with:

- tense;
- unrelated participles; or
- an ambiguous use of pronouns.

These are all explained below.

Wrong tense or tense inconsistency

Tense is the aspect of a verb that deals with time. It is possible to use more than one tense in one sentence, as in this:

> My father **was** a sheet-metal worker, I **am** a teacher and my daughter **is going to be** a teacher.

The first verb, *was*, is a form of the past tense; the second, *am*, is a form of the present; the third, *is going to be*, is a form of the future tense.

Other forms of the past include *has been*, *used to be*. Other forms of the present include *am being* (with verbs other than **be**, the present can also use *do*, as in *do like*, *do care*, etc.). Other forms of the future include *will be*.

There is no problem with the use of different tenses in that simple sentence. That is because the meaning of the sentence really is about different times so it is right to use different tenses. The key to all this is to keep a close eye on what you mean to write, what tense fits what you are trying to say. Keep rereading and checking! If you do, you are less likely to use tenses inconsistently, the commonest failing with this aspect of written grammar.

> **HINT** Over time, you will strengthen your grasp of tense if you read fairly quickly. Slow readers – and writers – easily lose track of what happens when.

> Shahida began his book at half-term and **finishes** it last week.

should be:

> Shahida began his book at half-term and **finished** it last week.

Began and *finished* are both verbs in the past tense. That fits the meaning of the sentence and is therefore consistent. It would also be consistent if the truth was this:

> Shahida began his book at half-term and will finish it next week.

There, *began* is in the past tense and *will finish* is in the future tense but the sentence is grammatically consistent because it fits the meaning.

A sentence such as:

*The staff will have written their reports by Friday and so **met** the deadline.*

should be:

*The staff will have written their reports by Friday and so **will meet** the deadline.*

In the first sentence, the staff have not yet completed the reports so it is not true to say they have already met a deadline. That does not make sense and so is inconsistent.

Unrelated participles

What are participles and in what ways might they be unrelated? In a sentence such as:

The school had closed for Easter.

the word *closed* follows a subject, the noun *school*, and immediately follows a form of the verb *to have*. A word that could do that is a **participle**, a part of the verb which expresses tense (in this case, a form of the past tense). Past participles often end in *-ed* but may end in *-en* (*written*), *-n* (*shown*), *-d* (*read*) or *-t* (*thought*).

In a sentence such as:

The school is closing for Easter.

the word *closing* follows a subject, the noun *school*, and immediately follows a form of the verb *to be*. Therefore, *closing* is also a participle and it expresses a form of the present tense.

A participle never has a subject, such as the pronouns *I, you, she, he, it, we, they*, immediately before it; the verb *to be* or *to have* has to come between them, as in the examples above.

Participles can be found in some clauses of this type:

Collaborating with someone who has more competence, a learner can be helped to construct new meanings.

In that sentence, the question of who does the *collaborating* is answered by the subject of the next clause: *the learner*. That is an example of a *related participle*; the participle is unambiguously related to a subject. However, the participle is not related to the subject in a sentence like this:

Collaborating with someone who has more competence, the teacher can help the learner to construct new meanings.

Here, the subject of that second clause is the teacher but the person who collaborates with someone who has more competence is the learner. The participle, *collaborating*, is *unrelated* to the subject, *the teacher*.

Unrelated participles are unacceptable because they are confusing and may be ambiguous. They should be avoided.

The sentence:

> *Being well-managed, the head of Armitage School could afford to employ a 0.5 teaching assistant after Christmas.*

is unacceptable because it is the school that is well-managed, not the head. The sentence:

> *Providing far more than the national average of free dinners, Seddon Junior School might be expected to have considerable problems.*

is acceptable because there is no doubt that it is the school that provides many free dinners.

Attachment ambiguities

Always keep an eye on the meaning of what you write or read. This book stresses that again and again but it is clear from what many people write that this advice is easily overlooked.

For example, if you wrote:

> *The headteacher told me about the exclusion appeal.*

you could add to that sentence a phrase about when the appeal was to be held. Where would that phrase appear? If you wrote:

> **On Monday,** *the headteacher told me about the exclusion appeal.*

that states unambiguously that Monday was the day that you were told. If you wrote:

> *The headteacher told me about the exclusion appeal* **on Monday.**

the change of position now *implies* that the appeal will take place on Monday. The problem is that it still allows the reader to *infer* that Monday was when you heard about the appeal. Does the phrase **on Monday** refer to the verb *told* or to the noun *appeal*? One sentence has two possible meanings although one – the timing of the appeal – is the more likely because *appeal* and *on Monday* appear close to each other.

It is easy to avoid this ambiguity by turning that added two-word phrase into a clause, as in:

> *The headteacher told me about the exclusion appeal* **that would take place on Monday.**

Vague or ambiguous pronoun reference

This kind of ambiguity is very common. In children's writing, it is very common indeed. One of the best activities that teachers can demonstrate, model and encourage is how to redraft a piece of writing by checking that there is no ambiguity about which nouns the pronouns refer to. Unless children (and other writers!) write quickly enough to be able to keep in mind what they are writing as they write, and unless they check what they write, it is very likely that they will use pronouns such as *he, she, it, they* (and the other forms of the pronoun, such as *him, her, them,* etc.) in ways that do not refer clearly to their nouns.

> *All the new computers and most of the stationery materials have been stored in the old stock cupboards. Nothing more can be done with **them** until the electrician arrives.*

should be:

> *All the new computers and most of the stationery materials have been stored in the old stock cupboards. Nothing more can be done with the computers until the electrician arrives.*

Unless the computers are specified – and that means using the noun, not the pronoun – it seems as if the electrician has to do something with the stationery as well. This would be, at least, confusing.

Clarity matters and, therefore, so does explicitness: that means using nouns instead of pronouns if it would be confusing to do otherwise.

> *Liam and Aloysius took Ryan and Nathan to see if **their** food was ready.*

should be:

> *Liam and Aloysius took Ryan and Nathan to see if all their food was ready.*

or:

> *Liam and Aloysius took Ryan and Nathan to see if Liam's and Aloysius' food was ready.*

or:

> *Liam and Aloysius took Ryan and Nathan to see if Ryan's and Nathan's food was ready.*

Which you use depends on your meaning. Some of these seem clumsy but even clumsiness is better than confusion. This particular confusion is very common in children's writing.

Confusion of words, e.g. imply/infer

All varieties of all languages change all the time. That is the single most obvious fact about language. Using Standard English does not mean using the language of a century or two ago if it is very different from usage today. On the other hand, many older usages are still widespread among literate users of English so you are advised still to follow that variety of Standard English.

One usage that seems to be common can cause real problems with understanding. English has many words that look and sound rather alike and so are sometimes used interchangeably but their meanings are quite different. If you say to a fairly educated person that you are *disinterested* about the children you teach, you should get some approval because it means that you are impartial, not that you are uninterested. So:

> *Just because I said I didn't mind teaching either Y3 or Y4, the headteacher thinks I'm* **disinterested**.

should be:

> *Just because I said I didn't mind teaching either Y3 or Y4, the headteacher thinks I'm* **uninterested**.

If you have no great preference, you really are *disinterested*!

The words *infer* and *imply* are more often misused than not. *Infer* is used far more often than *imply* and often it is used wrongly.

> *He* **inferred** *that I'm not bothered who I teach.*

should be:

> *He* **implied** *that I'm not bothered who [to be formal, whom] I teach.*

The odd thing about this particular confusion is that the words are almost opposite. If you imply something to a friend, your friend should infer the same message from you. *Infer* means *conclude*, as in:

> *From the way he was talking about falling numbers, I* **inferred** *that there could be a redundancy soon.*

Imply means to *suggest something without directly saying so*, as in:

> *I know she didn't say definitely but she* **implied** *that she might have a job for me next term.*

Here are some other words that are often confused:

Except in uncommon usages such as: *The staff room had been burgled when someone* **effected** *an entry from the playground side*, the word **effect** is used as a noun:

> *Unexpectedly, the music had a calming* **effect** *on a usually unruly class.*

Affect is almost always a verb, as in:

> *Yes, the music definitely* **affected** *them strongly.*

Rebut, **refute** and **deny** are sometimes used as though they were interchangeable. Their meanings are related but distinct:

> *When I implied that the deputy had forgotten about the Theatre in Education visit, she* **refuted** *what I had said by showing me the letter she had written to book the visit.*

Here, the deputy head proved that the implied accusation was wrong by providing evidence; she *refuted* it.

*She was angry and **rebutted** the accusation, calling me a nasty-minded trouble-maker who should think about a suitable job, such as pig-farming.*

The deputy is over emotional and does not bother with the evidence.

*All she needed to do was to **deny** it.*

The accuser now wishes that the deputy had restricted herself to a mere denial, without proving the point and without the anger. *Deny* can be an angry verb and it can involve proof but something else has to be added to make those points: *denied angrily, denied the accusation and showed the proof.*

Here are some other words that may get confused:

Discrete means separate, individually distinct, discontinuous (OED) not continuous; **discreet** means able to avoid embarrassing others – or yourself:

*Some of his sentences were a list of **discrete** words, unconnected by any grammatical device.*

but:

*There was so much rumour in the air that we all appreciated having such a **discreet** colleague.*

Accept means to receive something, particularly without fuss; **except** means that somebody or something is not part of a general situation:

*The head **accepted** my apology and carried on conducting the assembly himself.*

but:

*After the staff meeting, the head dismissed everybody **except** me.*

Contemptuous means that the subject feels contempt for somebody or something; **contemptible** is what that somebody or something is:

*My tutor was quite **contemptuous** of my efforts.*

but:

*Privately, even I had to agree that they really were **contemptible**.*

Militate means to have an influence against some evidence; **mitigate** means to reduce an effect, to soften or to appease:

*The latest SATs results **militate** against the last inspection report.*

but:

*The clarity and liveliness of Jeannie's story **mitigated** her general performance in school.*

Continuous means that something is without a break; *continual* means that something happens regularly:

> *On their way to the swimming baths, the class walked in a **continuous** line.*

but:

> *There is a **continual** outburst of delight every Friday.*

Different means that *this* is not like *that*; *differing* means that opinions or evidence clash:

> *This year's Y6 class is quite **different** from last year's.*

but:

> *The staff sat in silence as the **differing** views of the headteacher and her deputy thickened the air of the tiny staff room.*

Allusion means a rather indirect reference to something that you probably know about; *illusion* means an idea that does not fit reality:

> *Without mentioning any names or any events, the head made an **allusion** to the incident at the outdoor pursuits centre that lost the school its best speller.*

but:

> *The miscalculated test results caused us to live in a happy **illusion** until the SATs brought in reality.*

Stationary means without movement; *stationery* means paper, pens, etc.:

> *Luckily, the class knew they had to be quite **stationary** before crossing a busy road.*

but:

> *We were distraught by the lack of paper until the **stationery** supplies arrived.*

It helps to use a dictionary often, for spellings, for meanings – especially shades of meaning – and simply to get into the habit of using a valuable source of information. Other books, such as Bill Bryson's *Troublesome Words*, may also help.

Professional suitability and style

All native users of a language learn, from their earliest experiences of it, to match their style to their audience, to their own purpose in speaking or writing and to the topic being discussed. This test is about your ability to tell the difference between appropriate and inappropriate style. In particular, try to avoid these stylistic usages:

Non-parallelism in lists
When you write a list, look at the words you use to introduce the list. Each item in the list should follow grammatically from that introduction:

In future planning, I should remember to:

a. *to plan who should be in each group;*
b. *friendship groups.*

should be:

In future planning, I should remember to:

a. *plan who should be in each group;*
b. *consider friendship groups.*

No native user of English would say or write:

In future planning, I should remember to to plan who should be in each group.

or:

In future planning, I should remember to friendship groups.

Inconsistent register and tone

We can make a mistake with the tone of what we write. This is usually because we use a tone that is too formal or one that is too informal. Most writing is formal so a formal style is more appropriate in most cases.

An inconsistent style can show itself in the use of colloquialisms:

*It was reported last night that the Secretary of State was **doing her nut** over the slow progress of her latest initiative for small rural schools.*

The opening phrase, *'It was reported'*, implies that the speaker was a newsreader and the intended audience the general public. *'Doing her nut'* is inappropriate in a news report. The tone and style should be appropriate to the audience.

This would be more consistent in tone if it was written like this:

*It was reported last night that the Secretary of State was **concerned** over the slow progress of her latest initiative for small rural schools.*

An inconsistency of tone can also be created by mixing the use of active and passive constructions in the same sentence:

*Some of the children **opened** [active] the letters for home, **read** [active] them and **were torn up** [passive].*

should be either:

*Some of the children **opened** [active] the letters for home, **read** [active] them and **tore them up** [active].*

or:

> *Some of the letters for home **were opened** [passive] by the children, **read** [passive] and **torn up** [passive].*

In this last example, the auxiliary verb *were* has been left out from *were read* and *were torn up*. That is another case of *ellipsis*, what Dan Slobin calls *optional deletion*.

Finally, an inconsistent tone can also be created by mixing the use of the informal **you** and the more formal **one** in the same sentence. **You** is almost universal in speech, in sentences such as:

> *You never can tell.*

You is also appropriate in writing, especially informal writing; it is also appropriate in fairly formal writing. What is inappropriate is to mix the two styles:

> *Since **you** played such an active role in last year's Easter Fair, **one** should take up the challenge again this year.*

should be:

> *Since **you** played such an active role in last year's Easter Fair, **you** should take up the challenge again this year.*

On the other hand:

> *Although **you** always found that the middle term used to be the most productive, **one** finds the level of production more evenly spread over the year now.*

should be:

> *Although **one** always found that the middle term used to be the most productive, **one** finds the level of production more evenly spread over the year now.*

or:

> *Although **I** always found that the middle term used to be the most productive, **I** find the level of production more evenly spread over the year now.*

Both *one* and *you* can mean *people in general* or *people like us* or *me*. *You* can sometimes be confusing if it both carries that very general meaning and also means the other person. In other words, *you* is usually a second person pronoun, coming between *I* and *she/he/it*, and it can be confusing if it is used as a third person pronoun like *one*.

Be consistent.

Shift in person within sentences or across sentences
This is related to the last point above. Like that, it is related to what happens when formal and informal styles or register get mixed. It is also related to *cohesion* and the use

of pronouns. If you mean the same people, do not confuse things by referring to them as *you* when you really mean *they*:

> *Too many **people** are leaving doors open when **you** shouldn't.*

should be:

> *Too many **people** are leaving doors open when **they** shouldn't.*

or:

> *Too many **of you** are leaving doors open when **you** shouldn't.*

> ***One** hopes that the new community room will be ready before next term begins so that **we** can make full use of it.*

should be:

> ***We** hope that the new community room will be ready before next term begins so that **we** can make full use of it.*

Many problems with writing can be reduced greatly if you get into and keep the habit of reading what you write as you write it, rereading chunks and checking it at the end. Keep an eye on what you mean to say.

Excessive length and rambling sentences

This issue is related to earlier ones about abandoned constructions and failures to observe sentence boundaries. The key point is to see if very long sentences can be rewritten as more than one sentence. Long sentences are more than acceptable but only if the writer can control them:

> *Charlie is obviously a child that although has developed a high level of phonic under-standing and is capable of breaking down unknown words is still with my regards to the definition of a reader not successful.*

should be:

> *Charlie obviously has a high level of phonic understanding. He is able to break down unknown words. However, he is still not a successful reader in my view.*

The uncorrected sentence above is a genuine product of a trainee teacher. So is the following sentence:

> *With certain aspects of literacy I agree with Yetta Goodman (1980) whose research indicated that literacy is a naturally occurring and developing process in 'our liter-ate society', however, this development is minimal in comparison with the expected requirements, for example children may naturally occur certain literacy skills.*

should be:

Concerning certain aspects of literacy, I agree with Yetta Goodman (1980) whose research indicated that literacy is a naturally occurring and developing process in our literate society. This development is minimal in comparison with the expected requirements. For example, children may naturally acquire certain literacy skills.

You might have noticed that the uncorrected version has other problems, unconnected with sentence length or boundary. Problems rarely come singly.

Redundancy/tautology

If an expression means what you want to say, there is no need to add to it. It would make no sense to refer to the *STA Agency* because the acronym means *Standards and Testing Agency*.

*The headteacher reported that the governing body had **definitely** excluded Aloysius.*

should be:

The headteacher reported that the governing body had excluded Aloysius.

Exclusion is itself a word with no limits so there is no point in saying that it is *definite*.

Some kinds of apparent redundancy are more problematic. One change in Standard English over recent decades is that the verb *check* has almost been replaced by *check out*. They mean the same but it could be argued that the apparently redundant *out* is now part of a developing Standard English.

Inappropriate conjunctions (also known as connectives)

Look at what was said above about relative pronouns and relative clauses in 'Problems with relative pronouns in subordinate clauses'. Clauses that begin with *who, whom, which, that* are in a different category from those that begin with one of the long list of connectives such as *if, because, unless, so that, in case, although*, etc. All these words can begin a subordinate clause but the relationship with the main clause is different.

*The trouble with Roy is **because** he will not buckle down to hard work.*

should be:

*The trouble with Roy is **that** he will not buckle down to hard work.*

or:

*There is trouble with Roy **because** he will not buckle down to hard work.*

Some problems occur because the main clause has been completed and there seems to be a break in the writer's thinking before continuing with the subordinate clause:

*Roy's improvement has been **so** dramatic **so that** he could be quite near the top this year.*

should be:

*Roy's improvement has been dramatic **so** he could be quite near the top this year.*

or:

*Roy's improvement has been **so** dramatic **that** he could be quite near the top this year.*

Some conjunctions occur not only between clauses but also between phrases and even between single words. The problem is that sometimes these necessary words get left out:

The headteacher received a long silence at the staff meeting when he announced his intention to sing dance at the interval during the Christmas play.

should be:

*The headteacher received a long silence at the staff meeting when he announced his intention to sing **and** dance at the interval during the Christmas play.*

Remember that you will not be tested on all the items in this section nor is this list a syllabus. A glance at the sheer bulk of any grammar text should remind you that this is not exhaustive.

If you get stuck at any point, reread what you have done, ask if it makes clear sense and see if it is as consistent with the rest of the sentence, paragraph or text as you can make it.

Questions

In the Grammar section of the computerised test you will be shown part of a sentence and then presented with a range of optional clauses or phrases that might complete the sentence. You will have to decide which would be the correct option to complete the sentence grammatically and drag it into the space provided. The questions (usually between 3 or 4) will be selected from the 24 topics in the table on page 57. No tests are identical, so it would be wise to make sure you are familiar with all 24 issues!

The computerised test assesses your knowledge about grammar and your ability to detect when something is wrong. The Grammar test in this book involves you in precisely the same kind of thinking as the computerised test.

Below are three tests of your ability to detect:

- unrelated participles;
- the wrong tense or tense inconsistency;
- any lack of agreement between subject and verb.

Unrelated participles

In the following tests, tick the one option that seems to you to be **appropriate in its use of a related participle rather than an unrelated one.**

Questions

TEST A

Realising the role that speech plays in helping children to solve practical tasks,

1. it follows that children should be given tasks that require talk. ☐

2. Vygotsky placed language at the centre of all learning. ☐

3. language was seen by Vygotsky as central to learning. ☐

4. children's unassisted work is stressed by many teachers. ☐

TEST B

Persuaded by her staff that afternoon playtimes were increasingly disruptive,

1. the head decided to have no playtimes in the afternoon but to end school ten minutes early. ☐

2. afternoon play was abandoned by the head and replaced with an earlier hometime. ☐

3. the school exchanged its afternoon play for a shorter afternoon session. ☐

4. the children had no play but could leave school ten minutes earlier. ☐

TEST C

1. The curriculum, according to Peters, is not wholly an end in itself, conceding that even history can be viewed in an instrumental way. ☐

2. Peters believes that the curriculum is not wholly an end in itself, conceding that even history can be viewed in an instrumental way. ☐

3. Conceding that even history can be viewed in an instrumental way, the view that the curriculum is an end in itself is not fully supported by Peters. ☐

4. Conceding that even history can be viewed in an instrumental way, Peters' view of the curriculum is not wholly in favour of education as an end in itself. ☐

TEST D

Thought to be the easiest class in the school to teach,

1. the head was surprised by the mayhem they caused during silent reading. ☐

2. it was surprising to the head that they could cause so much mayhem during silent reading. ☐

3. the mayhem they caused during silent reading was a surprise for the head. ☐

4. the children caused mayhem during silent reading. ☐

Wrong tense or tense inconsistency

In the following tests, tick the one option that seems to you to be **appropriate in its use of the right and most consistent tense.**

TEST A

Although I wish now that I had worked harder, my A level results were very pleasing and it has meant

1. being able to be more ambitious in the applications I made. ☐

2. that I have been able to be more ambitious in the applications I made. ☐

3. that I was able to be more ambitious in the applications I made. ☐

4. that I am able to be more ambitious in the applications I made. ☐

TEST B

I don't consider myself a very gifted person, although I did well enough, but my headteacher father believes I'll make a good teacher and that, although I have always been a little naïve,

1. life was good. ☐

2. life being good. ☐

3. life is good. ☐

4. life will be good. ☐

TEST C

Whatever I do, my mind fills with thoughts of what could happen if I chose a course where I can't fit in, the other students don't respond, the staff are cold and unhelpful and my tutor

1. is bad-tempered. ☐

2. was bad-tempered. ☐

3. has been bad-tempered. ☐

4. being bad-tempered. ☐

Questions

TEST D

Perhaps the best action for me to take is to talk with friends, at least once I have examined what different areas offer, compared facilities, accommodation and opportunities and

1. growing a little more sure of myself. ☐

2. grow a little more sure of myself. ☐

3. grew a little more sure of myself. ☐

4. grown a little more sure of myself. ☐

Lack of agreement between subject and verb

In the following tests, tick the one option that seems to you to be **appropriate in its agreement between subject and verb**.

TEST A

The trouble with both the way I talk and the way I write

1. are ☐
2. were ☐ that for
3. was ☐
4. is ☐

much of the time I cannot trust myself to remember what I started with.

TEST B

A friend told me that the likeliest cause of this problem is that the unrelentingly abusive attitudes shown by my first English teacher

1. is quite traumatic for me. ☐

2. were quite traumatic for me. ☐

3. was quite traumatic for me. ☐

4. being quite traumatic for me. ☐

TEST C

I wish it were that simple. In fact,

1. are ☐
2. were ☐
3. was ☐
4. is ☐

it that teacher, the one who helped

me to qualify for university, the sicknesses I had as a child or my supportive but rather

TEST D

As I look ahead, I know that the future, whether I am lucky or not or leave teaching or stay with it, and whatever anyone else does or says,

1. was mine to make. ☐

2. has been mine to make. ☐

3. will be mine to make. ☐

4. will have been mine to make. ☐

3.5 Comprehension

Introduction

8–12 marks are available for comprehension.

Most of the test is about writing. This section is about reading.

Teachers now have to read a great deal of written material about their professional lives and work. This material can be government documents (for example, on the law concerning exclusion from school), the educational press and very frequent information about the local educational scene. Because every teacher now has to do so much professionally demanding reading, there is a greater stress than there was previously on their being able to:

*   identify the key points in a text;
*   'read between the lines' in order to make inferences and deductions;
*   differentiate between fact and fiction in a written text;
*   understand which points are more significant than others and how this relative importance affects a text;
*   comprehend a text well enough to be able to re-present the meaning in a different way from the original;
*   retrieve factual information and/or specific ideas from a text;
*   judge whether specific comments made about a text are actually supported, implied, implicitly or explicitly contradicted, or simply not present in that text;
*   summarise information from a section, or about a topic, in a text;
*   identify or adapt suitable information from a text for a specific audience.

The test will expect you to be sufficiently proficient in these skills in order to complete the following tasks:

- attribute statements to categories;
- complete a bulleted list;
- sequence information;
- present main points;
- match texts to summaries;
- identify the meanings of words and phrases;
- evaluate statements about the text;
- select headings and subheadings;
- identify possible readership or audience for a text.

These are the nine possible comprehension question types.

The test you take will test only a selection of these aspects of literacy.

The comprehension test presents candidates with a short text and a series of questions on it. Read the whole text first. Good reading means paying almost simultaneous attention to the word or phrase you are concentrating on at the time and also to as much of the whole text as you have read and can keep in mind. To do this test well, you will need to focus on what is significant in the whole text so that you are able to select those bits and ignore the rest. Some questions ask you to see how this bit of the text relates to that bit, to notice how parts of the text are organised, to sequence ideas and to check what some phrases or words mean in the context. None of this is extraordinary and an attentive and reasonably experienced reader should not have difficulties.

Questions

There are nine possible comprehension question types; each Literacy Skills Test will test a selection of these. However, for the sake of this exercise, tasks have been set using all nine comprehension question types.

Read this extract from an Ofsted document and complete the following tasks.

Ofsted to revise the framework for initial teacher education (ITE)

Ofsted is proposing to raise expectations of providers of teacher training to help ensure that more trainees are better prepared with the practical skills that teachers need most, such as the ability to manage behaviour and teach reading effectively.

Feedback on the current inspection arrangements has been positive but also suggests the need to continue to raise expectations. This means drawing up clearer, more challenging criteria with fewer, more streamlined judgements and one overarching judgement for overall effectiveness. Ofsted is also seeking views on reducing the eight-week notice period for an inspection to three weeks.

Questions

Her Majesty's Chief Inspector (HMCI) of Education said, 'The quality of teaching is an essential element in any school so the selection and training of the next generation of teachers is crucial. We hope that changes to the way we inspect initial teacher education will enable inspectors to focus even more on the things that are important: teaching pupils to read, behaviour management and trainees' ability to teach a range of learners, including those with special educational needs and/or disabilities.

'Inspection helps to raise standards and ensure the best training is provided. We want more trainees to become good or outstanding teachers and gain employment in schools. This is why, in the new arrangements, we want to focus inspection afresh on observing current and former trainees in the classroom. I'd like to encourage anyone with an interest in initial teacher education, in particular those who provide training, are currently in training, or thinking of joining a teacher training programme, to tell us their views.'

Building on the strengths of the current arrangements, it is proposed that inspection will look more closely at the selection of trainees and the quality of partnerships ITE providers have with settings, schools and colleges. It will focus even more on the quality of training and trainees' subject knowledge and their understanding and competence in developing pupils' literacy skills, including using systematic phonics to teach reading. Ofsted is also considering incorporating a thematic element into inspections, on a rolling programme, in order to gain more evidence on the effectiveness of training to teach specific subjects and aspects such as managing behaviour.

The proposals include a more proportionate approach to inspection that is informed by a robust risk assessment process so inspections can be targeted where improvement is needed most. Partnerships previously judged to be satisfactory will be inspected at an early stage in the new cycle and those that continue to be satisfactory will be subject to a monitoring inspection, which will take place 12–18 months after the inspection. Finally, a full inspection is likely to take place within three years of the previous inspection.

Ofsted proposes that initial teacher education inspections will also:

- retain the focus on trainees' outcomes at the heart of the inspection
- be underpinned by clear and more challenging criteria for judging partnerships to be outstanding or good
- take account of the views of users, trainees and former trainees, including newly qualified and recently qualified teachers
- use an on-line questionnaire to gather the views of trainees
- integrate judgements on equality and diversity throughout the report, including reporting on the performance of different groups of trainees
- introduce a focused monitoring inspection; for example, to look at the provision of phonics training where newly qualified teacher feedback raises concerns

Questions

- *continue to involve leaders, managers, tutors, mentors, trainees and former trainees in discussions during an inspection*
- *continue to take account of a partnership's self-evaluation, and*
- *continue to drive improvement in the sector by providing an external evaluation of strengths and weaknesses.*

The proposals take into account feedback from providers, inspectors and other stakeholders with an interest in ITE.

Attributing statements to categories

Read the statements below and decide which refer to:

ITEP   Initial Teacher Education Providers

TT   Trainee Teachers

O   Ofsted

HMCI   Her Majesty's Chief Inspector

Put the correct code in the box to the left of each statement.

(In the computerised test, you will be asked to drag the code to the box.)

☐	They are going to require more from teacher training courses.
☐	They regard the training of the next cohort of teachers as very significant.
☐	They are going to be expected to know how to develop literacy skills.
☐	They are going to have to look more closely at placements.

Completing a bulleted list

Look at the phrases below. Put a tick next to the three that most accurately complete the stem. The final one has been done for you.

(In the computerised test you will be asked to drag a number of phrases one at a time to the bulleted list.)

It is anticipated that all future ITE inspections will:

-

-

-

- **continue to take account of a partnership's self-evaluation.**

☐ target inspections only where improvement is most needed

☐ focus entirely on specific themes such as behaviour management

☐ be strengthened by tougher criteria for judging outstanding or good trainees

☐ be preceded by a notice period of only three weeks

☐ improve ITE by providing an external evaluation of strengths and weaknesses

☐ gauge the diversity of partnerships ITE providers have established

☐ be reinforced by a more demanding measure of outstanding or good partnerships

☐ take account of the views of newly or recently qualified teachers

Sequencing information

From the seven statements below select the three that most accurately reflect the order of the steps to be taken in the new cycle of inspection of the partnerships ITE providers have with their settings, schools and colleges.

Write FIRST, SECOND OR THIRD in the box to the left of your choice of statement.

(In the computerised test you will be asked to click on the labels FIRST, SECOND or THIRD, one at a time, and drag them to the boxes beside your chosen answer.)

☐ All partnerships will undergo an initial risk assessment.

☐ Partnerships previously judged to be satisfactory will be inspected.

☐ Those showing most need for improvement will be inspected first.

☐ All partnerships will be inspected within three years of this revision.

☐ Those that continue to be satisfactory will be inspected within 12 to 18 months.

☐ Partnerships will have a full inspection within three years of a previous inspection.

☐ Partnerships' chances of being inspected will be proportionate to their quality.

Presenting main points

From the list below, select the four points that most accurately describe Ofsted's main objectives in revising the inspection framework for ITE. Tick the box to the left of the point to indicate your four choices.

Questions

(In the computerised test you will be asked to click on your four choices, one at a time, and drag them to four empty bullet points in the adjacent box.)

☐ Gauge the effectiveness of the teaching of phonics by newly qualified teachers.

☐ Look more closely at how trainees are evaluated and selected for ITE.

☐ Scrutinise the inspection criteria used to assess teachers in schools.

☐ Encourage teachers working in schools to tell them their views on ITE.

☐ Upgrade the quality of training given by ITE providers.

☐ Ensure practical teaching skills are top of the agenda for trainees.

☐ Introduce a thematic approach into the inspection of behaviour management.

☐ Introduce one comprehensive criterion for the general effectiveness of ITE provision.

☐ Reduce the notice period given prior to inspection of ITE provision.

Matching texts to summaries

Reread paragraphs 1, 3 and 5. From the list of statements below, select the one that most accurately summarises the content of these three paragraphs. Tick the box next to your choice.

(In the computerised test you will be asked to drag a tick symbol to the box beside your choice.)

☐ It is vital to build on the strengths of the current arrangements and raise the expectations of the next generation of trainee teachers.

☐ It is time for a complete overhaul of the inspection process for ITE so that schools can focus even more on the things that are important.

☐ The most important attributes of the trainee teacher emerging from ITE are the abilities to control and manage behaviour and to teach literacy effectively.

☐ Teaching can be improved by raising expectations, introducing a more rigorous selection of trainees and improving the quality of settings, schools and colleges.

Identifying the meanings of words and phrases

Select the most suitable alternative for the phrase as it appears in the context of the passage. Tick the box next to your choice.

Questions

(In the computerised test you will be asked to drag a tick symbol to the box beside your choice.)

'... raise expectations of providers of teacher training' (paragraph 1) is closest in meaning to:

☐   investigate the endeavours of providers of teacher training

☐   lift the requirements of providers of teacher training

☐   boost the hopes of providers of teacher training

☐   increase the demands on providers of teacher training

'... a more proportionate approach to' (paragraph 6) is closest in meaning to:

☐   a more commensurate method of

☐   a more detached pathway to

☐   a more competitive move towards

☐   a more rigorous course of

Evaluating statements about the text

Read each of the statements below about the Ofsted revision of the framework for initial teacher education and decide which of them:

is supported by the text	**S**
is implied to be the case, or implicitly supported, by the text	**I**
states something for which there is no evidence or support in the text	**NE**
is implicitly contradicted or implicitly refuted in the text	**IC**
is explicitly contradicted or refuted in the text.	**EC**

Put the appropriate code in the box alongside each statement.

(In the computerised test you will be asked to drag the code to the appropriate answer.)

Questions

 The views of trainee teachers are not being sought at this stage.

Many trainee teachers feel they have not been fully prepared with the essential practical skills for teaching.

Inspection helps to raise standards and ensure that the best training is given.

  Some new teachers are not as good at managing behaviour as they should be.

The present system for the selection of trainees is satisfactory.

Selecting headings and subheadings

From the four options below, choose the most suitable subheading for the second half of the text to be inserted at the top of paragraph 5. Tick the box next to your choice of subheading.

(*In the computerised test you will be asked to drag a tick to your choice of answer.*)

Selecting for quality

Going from strength to strength

Need for a fresh focus

Calling all teachers

Identifying possible readership or audience for a text

From the list of possible audiences for this document, select the audience that you think it would be most relevant to, and put an **M** in the box alongside; and the one you think it would be least relevant to, and put an **L** in the box alongside.

(*In the computerised test you will be asked to drag an **M** for the most relevant audience, or an **L** for the least relevant audience, into the appropriate boxes.*)

  Headteachers in primary schools

Institutions providing initial teacher training

Teachers of English in primary schools

Qualified teachers working in schools

Remember: only three of these nine aspects of literacy will appear in the actual test.

3.6 Answers and key points

Spelling

1. *independent*

Key points
Most words that end with that sound end in *-ent*.

2. demonstrable

Key points
Some words, like *demonstrate, educate,* lose an element when they gain a suffix.

3. *assessment*

Key points
Words vary in the way that they spell the *s* sound. This word has two pairs of doubles.

4. adolescence

Key points
Words vary in the way they spell the *s* sound. This word uses *sc.*

5. *pursue*

Key points
The sound represented here by *ur* is represented by different letter-strings in other words. They simply have to be learned by heart.

6. *fairies*

Key points
Luckily, this is one of the most reliable rules. Nouns that end in a consonant and *-y,* such as *fairy, party*, etc., drop the *y* and add *-ies* in the plural form.

Answers

7. *weighing*

Key points
This is clear but complex. If the sound is *ee*, the rule for using *i* and *e* together really is '*ie* except after *c*'. If the sound is not *ee*, the *e* comes first.

8. *fuelled*

Key points
Verbs that end in a single *-l*, like *instil*, take a second *l* when either *-ed* or *-ing* is added.

9. *affected*

Key points
The distinction between *affect* and *effect* baffles many educated adults. If you *affect* something, you have an *effect* on it. Try that as a mnemonic, with the *a* of *affect* coming first, as in the alphabet.

10. *responsibility*

Key points
Another case of having to learn by heart. There are just two ways to spell the suffixes we find in *capable* and *terrible*. Of *-able*/*ible* and *ability*/*ibility*, *able*/*ability* is the more common.

11. *practice*

Key points
Practice/*practise* and *advice*/*advise* confuse a lot of us. The words ending in *-ice* are nouns and could have the word *the* before them; the words ending in *-ise* are verbs and could have the word *I* in front of them.

12. *disappear*

Key points
Morphology, the way that words are built up from their parts, helps here. The prefixes *mis-* and *dis-* end in a single *-s*. What follows is a stem word, like *-take* or *-appear*. Those who write *dissappear* have imagined a non-existent prefix *diss-*.

Answers

13. *possession*

Key points
Here, the sound *s* is represented twice by *ss*. The double *ss* is very likely in the middle of a word and quite likely at the end.

14. *impracticable*

Key points
This is a mixture of morphology and the need to learn by heart whether a word uses *-able* or *-ible*. The morphology involved is a series of prefix + stem + suffix: *im + practice + able*. *Practice* loses *e*; *able* changes.

15. *humorous*

Key points
The stem word, the abstract noun *humour*, drops the *u* when it adds the adjective suffix *-ous*. This happens in other words, such as *labour*, *laborious* (but notice the added *i* in *laborious*).

16. *exaggerated*

Key points
Remember that the commonest type of misspelling is the use or non-use of the double consonant (incidentally, notice that word *misspelling*). This is one of the hardest to remember because there are no analogies.

17. *regrettably*

Key points
This is not about *able/ible* but about the way that a verb that ends in a consonant such as t is likely to double that consonant when an adverb suffix, such as *-ably*, is added. There are also analogies with *forget*, *forgettably*.

18. *automatically*

Key points
Apart from the use of a Greek suffix, *auto-*, meaning *self*, it is also a case of a fairly long and complex word whose spelling is close to the way it is said.

Answers

19. *curriculum*

> **Key points**
> Another example of the double consonant; these words are best learned by heart.

20. *embarrassment*

> **Key points**
> A useful mnemonic with this word might be: He went **R**eally **R**ed and **S**miled **S**hyly with embaRRaSSment.

21. *pedagogy*

> **Key points**
> Meaning 'the science of teaching'. The origin is Greek: 'paidagagos' – the slave who took children to and from school. This is a spelling best learned by heart.

22. *allowed*

> **Key points**
> Confusion between such homophones as *allowed*, *a loud* and *aloud* is serious because it shows that the writer does very little reading and that the simple grammatical and meaning distinctions between the participle *allowed* and the adverb *aloud* have been overlooked.

23. *allot*

> **Key points**
> The words *allot* and *a lot* are also homophones; they sound the same as each other but have different meanings. We *allot* when we distribute something among recipients. There may be *a lot* of recipients.

24. *maturity*

> **Key points**
> It is another example of the way that an adjective, *mature*, drops the final *e* when the noun suffix *-ity* is added but it is also quite regular phonically.

Answers

25. *counselling*

Key points
The usual UK spelling is 'counselling'. While the US version, 'counseling', is acceptable, the misspellings in the question (counciling, counsiling, councelling) are incorrect. Most errors arise from the confusion of the words 'council' and 'counsel'.

26. *miscellaneous*

Key points
Notice the use of *sc* for the *s* sound, the double *ll* and the *e* in the final syllable. Also, its parts are *misc + ell + an + eous*.

27. *approximation*

Key points
The use of a double consonant is a frequent problem; the use of *x* is infrequent.

28. *reprehensible*

Key points
There are no double consonants but the use of *i* in the final consonant is fairly rare.

29. *apprenticeship*

Key points
Here, there is a double consonant; the *s* sound is represented by *ce*.

Punctuation

1. As soon as we speak, (1) we reveal a great deal of ourselves to our audience. Suppose you ask someone,

    (2) "Shall we have a drink? (3)" (4)

    Suppose the other person replies, (5)

    "Yes, I'd like a whiskey, (6) me."

    That tag, *me*, tells you that the speaker probably comes from (7) Manchester.

Answers

Sometimes, what people say does tell you something about their origin but it is less definite. A friend asks you and another friend,

"Now, what would youse two like to drink?"

The questioner may or may not come from Ireland but will certainly have a background there because that use of (8) 'youse', unknown in Standard English, has its roots in the Irish having one form of 'you' for one person (9) (tú) and another form of 'you' for two people (9) (sibh). However, (10) none of this means that any of these speakers could actually speak any Irish!

Key points

(1) The subordinate clause appears first so it should be separated from the main clause by a comma.

(2) The first letter in the sentence needs a capital letter.

(3) A question requires a question mark.

(4) Direct speech needs speech marks both at the beginning and at the end. The two marks, paired, form a consistency.

(5) The mark before a direct quotation is usually a comma.

(6) A comma is needed to separate the tag 'me' from the rest.

(7) The city of Manchester requires a capital letter.

(8) This is a bit of language that differs from the rest of the text and needs quotation marks to identify it.

(9) The Irish words tú and sibh break into the rest and are best placed within brackets.

(10) A comma is needed after 'However'. This is important because 'however' can have two different meanings:

  – nevertheless; yet; on the other hand; in spite of that

  – to whatever extent or degree; no matter how

The comma indicates the intended meaning. Consider the two sets of sentences below:

However the scripts were analysed, the marks remained the same.

However, the scripts were analysed; the marks remained the same.

Or

The marks remained the same however the scripts were analysed.

The marks remained the same; however, the scripts were analysed.

Answers

2. The concern of the (11) Head of (12) English was evident after reading the (13) 'Can do Better' report on literacy. If we look at (14) boys' performance in English, we have to agree that there is, generally (15), some cause for concern. Is there anything that can be done to help them improve?

Among the (16) short-term approaches that seemed to help boys are (17):

enthusiastically encouraged private reading;

clearly set tasks (18);

explicit teaching of reading strategies;

a wide range of outcomes from reading;

reading preferences that are discussed.

Key points

(11) and (12) As proper nouns, the head of english needs capital letters: 'Head of English'.

(13) The title of a document should be in single quotation marks.

(14) The performance belongs to the boys so an apostrophe is needed after the **s**.

(15) The interruption of the flow of the sentence by the word 'generally' should be marked by twinned commas, one before and one after the word.

(16) A hyphen should be used to link the two words to show they are one unit of meaning. Without a hyphen 'short term' could mean a school term of only a few weeks.

(17) A list is being introduced so a colon is necessary.

(18) Each item on the list is more than one word long and needs separating with a semicolon.

---

3. What is it about (19) Standard English that makes it standard? (20)

    (21)

    Like every language, English has gone through many changes. The Saxons and Angles who settled here brought their own languages with them, (22) predominantly Saxon, and after a while the dialects of Anglo-Saxon overcame the Celtic languages that had flourished along with Latin until soon after the Romans left in 410AD. The languages spoken by the later Scandinavian invaders were probably just about intelligible to some of the Anglo-(23)Saxons but changes and borrowings continued: the new invaders' (24) legacy to us includes *they, them, their*. Anglo-Saxon, modified by Scandinavian, with dialects that were barely intelligible to

Answers

other Anglo-Saxon speakers, continued for hundreds of years but, thankfully, (25) it became simpler. (26) The German word for *big* is *gross* but it has six versions. Our Anglo-Saxon ancestors had eleven versions of adjectives; (27) we have just three: *big*, *bigger*, *biggest*. Even when we complicate matters by having *good*, *better*, (28) *best*, that is still easier than Anglo-Saxon! (29)

Key points

(19) There is no need for a capital for *standard*; the lower case version is now the accepted convention.

(20) A question requires a question mark.

(21) After the first sentence, comes the beginning of an answer. A new paragraph is needed.

(22) *predominantly Saxon* breaks into the sentence and needs a pair of commas, one before and one after.

(23) A hyphen is needed for Anglo-Saxon (as for Irish-American).

(24) The noun is *invaders* so they need an apostrophe before *legacy*.

(25) *Thankfully* is also an interruption and a pair of commas is needed.

(26) A sentence ends with a full stop.

(27) There are two sentences but their meanings are so closely related that they need a semicolon to link them.

(28) The series of three items in a list without an *and* requires a series of commas.

(29) This is an exclamation but that shows how personal punctuation is.

Grammar

Unrelated participles

A 2 *Vygotsky* is the one who did the *realising*; who *realised*.

B 1 The *headteacher* was the one who was *persuaded*.

C 2 It was *Peters* who *conceded*, who did the *conceding*, not his views.

D 4 The *children were thought*, nobody and nothing else.

Key points

This relates to the issue of agreement between subject and verb. You clarify the matter by asking *who did* it.

Answers

Wrong tense or tense consistency
A   2

> **Key points**
> *have been* makes most sense because it matches or agrees with the other verbs: the series of *wish* and *had worked* followed by *were* and *has meant*. *Made* confirms the choice of *have been* because it makes *was* impossible.

B   4

> **Key points**
> When there are several verbs in a sentence, some in different tenses, the question is to decide what other verb this one should be like. This verb is part of a series beginning *I'll make* and so is in the future tense.

C   1

> **Key points**
> There is a series of short clauses beginning with *I can't* and all have to use the same verb form.

D   4

> **Key points**
> *grown* makes most sense because it is the only option that fits the use of the verb form *have examined*: *compared* parallels *grown* because the two verbs make use of the *have* of *have examined*.

Lack of agreement between subject and verb
A   4

> **Key points**
> The subject of the sentence is *trouble*, a singular noun, so the verb has to be singular also: *is*. There can often be a problem with subjects whose headwords are a long way from the verb; it is very easy to be trapped into picking up the nearest noun and thinking that that is the subject (in this sentence, the trap is *way*). This question does also ask you to be careful about the tense: the present.

Answers

B   2

> ### *Key points*
> The subject is *attitudes* so the verb has to be in the plural: *were*. Again, there is always a problem with a sentence with several nouns: out of *friend*, *cause*, *problem*, *attitudes*, *teacher*, which is the subject of this verb? The correct tense confirms the answer.

C   3

> ### *Key points*
> This seems quite easy but the issue is that there are, apparently, several subjects: *teacher*, *sicknesses*, *parents*. The clue is the word *or* which tells you, logically, that only one thing is the subject, not everything listed. This is confirmed by the singular *it*.

D   3

> ### *Key points*
> This time, the tense not only fits the grammar but also the obvious sense of *the future*.

Comprehension

Attributing statements to categories

 They are going to require more from teacher training courses.

> ### *Key points*
> Para 1 says that Ofsted is proposing to raise expectations of providers of teacher training.

 They regard the training of the next cohort of teachers as very significant.

> ### *Key points*
> Para 3 reports the HMCI saying that the training of the next generation of teachers is crucial.

Answers

TT

They are going to be expected to know how to develop literacy skills.

Key points
Para 5 says that inspections will focus even more on the quality of training and trainees' subject knowledge and their understanding and competence in developing pupils' literacy skills.

ITEP

They are going to have to look more closely at placements.

Key points
Para 5 says that inspection will concentrate on the quality of partnerships ITE providers have with settings, schools and colleges.

Completing a bulleted list
It is anticipated that all future ITE inspections will:

- take account of the views of newly or recently qualified teachers

Key points
Bullet point 3 says Ofsted proposes to take account of the views of users, trainees and former trainees, including newly qualified and recently qualified teachers

- target inspections only where improvement is most needed

Key points
Para 6 says Ofsted proposes that future inspections will be informed by a robust risk assessment process so they can be targeted where improvement is needed most.

- improve ITE by providing an external evaluation of strengths and weaknesses

Key points
Bullet point 9 says that Ofsted proposes to drive improvement in the sector by providing an external evaluation of strengths and weaknesses.

Answers

Sequencing information
FIRST Partnerships previously judged to be satisfactory will be inspected.

> #### Key points
> This is the first part of the new proportionate process described in paragraph 6.

SECOND Those that continue to be satisfactory will be inspected within 12 to 18 months.

> #### Key points
> This is the next step in the process.

THIRD Partnerships will have a full inspection within three years of a previous inspection.

> #### Key points
> This is the final stage of the new process.

Presenting main points
Upgrade the quality of training given by ITE providers.

> #### Key points
> Para 1 says that Ofsted is proposing to raise expectations of providers of teacher training.

Look more closely at how trainees are evaluated and selected for ITE.

> #### Key points
> Para 5 says that Ofsted proposes that inspection will look more closely at the selection of trainees.

Ensure practical teaching skills are top of the agenda for trainees.

> #### Key points
> Para 1 says that Ofsted is proposing to ensure that more trainees are better prepared with the practical skills that teachers need most. The point (about behaviour management) is then repeated three times elsewhere in the text.

Answers

Introduce one comprehensive criterion for the general effectiveness of ITE provision.

Key points
Para 2 says that clearer, more challenging criteria with fewer, more streamlined judgements and one overarching judgement for overall effectiveness are to be drawn up.

These points should **not** be included:

Encourage teachers working in schools to tell them their views on ITE.

Key points
Para 4 says HMCI would like 'in particular those who provide training, are currently in training, or thinking of joining a teacher training programme, to tell us their views'. This list does not include practising teachers.

Gauge the effectiveness of the teaching of phonics by newly qualified teachers.

Key points
Bullet point 6 suggests that inspections will look at the provision of phonics training received by trainees where their feedback raises concerns.

Introduce a thematic approach into the inspection of behaviour management.

Key points
Para 5 talks about a thematic element to inspection; not just about the inspection of behaviour management.

Scrutinise the inspection criteria used to assess teachers in schools.

Key points
The document concerns the scrutiny of teaching in ITE, not the teaching in schools.

Reduce the notice period given prior to inspection of ITE provision.

Key points
This is not a main objective; it is a topic on which Ofsted is seeking views.

Answers

Matching texts to summaries
Reread paragraphs 1, 3 and 5. From the list of statements below, select the one that most accurately summarises the content of these three paragraphs. Tick the box next to your choice. (*In the computerised test you will be asked to drag a tick symbol to the box beside your choice.*)

The most important attributes of the trainee teacher emerging from ITE are the abilities to control and manage behaviour and to teach literacy effectively.

> ### Key points
> When summarising the three paragraphs look for the key points they share. All three stress the importance of being able to manage behaviour and to teach literacy.

While the other statements are significant, they are not common to all three paragraphs and should not be chosen.

Identifying the meanings of words and phrases
'... **raise expectations of providers of teacher training**' (paragraph 1) is closest in meaning to:

investigate the endeavours of providers of teacher training

> ### Key points
> This is only a part of raising expectations. **Do not** choose this option.

lift the requirements of providers of teacher training

> ### Key points
> In this context 'requirements' and 'expectations' are very close in meaning. **This option should be selected.**

boost the hopes of providers of teacher training

> ### Key points
> In this context, 'boosting hopes' is not the same thing as 'raising expectations'. **Do not** choose this option.

Answers

increase the demands on providers of teacher training

Key points
Increasing demands is not the same thing as raising expectations; it is the result of raising expectations. **Do not** choose this option.

'... **a more proportionate approach to'** (paragraph 6) is closest in meaning to:

a more commensurate method of

Key points
The words 'commensurate' and 'proportionate' have a very similar meaning, i.e. that of 'balance' or 'equality' or 'levelness'. **This option should be selected.**

a more detached pathway to

Key points
The words 'detached' and 'proportionate' do not have the same meaning. **Do not** choose this option.

a more competitive move towards

Key points
In this context there is no defined competitor for inspection and this option should not be chosen. **Do not** choose this option.

a more rigorous course of

Key points
This means a tougher course of inspection; this does not have the same meaning as 'balanced' or 'in proportion'. **Do not** choose this option.

Evaluating statements about the text

 EC | The views of trainee teachers are not being sought at this stage.

Key points
Paragraph 4 states: 'I'd like to encourage anyone ... in particular ... those who are currently in training, ... to tell us their views.'

Answers

 NE Many trainee teachers feel they have not been fully prepared with the essential practical skills for teaching.

Key points
This does not appear in the text.

S Inspection helps to raise standards and ensure that the best training is given.

Key points
Paragraph 4 says that inspection helps to raise standards and ensure the best training is provided.

I Some new teachers are not as good at managing behaviour as they should be.

Key points
In four places the document states that classroom behaviour and management are issues that need to be addressed with a view to improvement. This implies that in some newly qualified teachers, these skills are lacking.

IC The present system for the selection of trainees is satisfactory.

Key points
Paragraph 5 opening sentence 'it is proposed that inspection will look more closely at the selection of trainees ...' Without actually saying as much, this contradicts the idea that the current system is satisfactory.

Selecting headings and subheadings
Selecting for quality

Key points
This is one of a number of important points in this section of the text. **Do not** choose it.

Answers

Going from strength to strength

Key points
This covers 'building on the strengths' (paragraph 5); 'retain the focus on trainees' outcomes'; continue to involve leaders et al. in inspections; and continue to drive improvement (bullet points). **This option should be selected.**

Need for a fresh focus

Key points
This is one of a number of proposals in the document; further, the need to 'focus afresh' is mentioned in the first half of the document (paragraph 4). **Do not** choose it.

Calling all teachers

Key points
This is a fairly minor point in the document first mentioned in paragraph 4. **Do not** choose it.

Identifying possible readership or audience for a text
Headteachers in primary schools

Key points
These headteachers might be interested but only if they were partnership schools or offering ITT training. **Do not** choose this option.

Institutions providing initial teacher training

Key points
These institutions are likely to be very interested as they are the subject of inspection. **Choose this audience as the 'most relevant' (M).**

Teachers of English in primary schools

Key points
These teachers might be interested especially in the references to literacy and phonics. However, they would not be directly affected by many of the other details. **Do not** choose this option.

Answers

Qualified teachers working in schools

Key points
These teachers are only very marginally affected by this review. The HMCI does not include them on the list of people involved in ITT from whom it would be interesting to hear and they are not directly mentioned in the text. **Choose this audience as the 'least relevant' (L).**

4 | The Numeracy Skills Test

4.1 Introduction

Introduction to the test

The numeracy skills test is a computerised test, which is divided into two sections:

- **section 1 for the mental arithmetic questions;**
- **section 2 for the written questions known as 'on-screen' questions.**

The **mental arithmetic** section is an audio test heard through headphones. Calculators are not allowed, but noting numbers and jotting down working will be permitted. (You will be issued with a wipe-clean board and a pen to help with this.) There are 12 questions in this section. Note: this section must be answered first; each question has a fixed time in which you must answer (18 seconds); you cannot return to a question if you later wish to change your answer. Questions will be asked to test your ability to carry out mental calculations using fractions, percentages, measurement, conversions and time (see the detailed content list on page 117).

The **'on-screen'** questions: there are 16 written questions in this section. Seven questions are focused on *interpreting* and using written data and nine are focused on *solving* written arithmetic problems. Questions and answers will be in one of the following forms:

- **multiple-choice questions where you will choose the single correct response from a fixed number of alternative answers;**
- **multiple-response questions where you choose single or multiple correct statements from a fixed number of given statements;**
- **questions that require a single answer;**
- **questions where you will select the answer by pointing and clicking on the correct point in a table, chart or graph (to change an answer click on an alternative point);**
- **questions where you will select your answer from a number of alternative answers and place the answer into the answer box provided (to change an answer drag it back to its original position and choose another).**

In this part of the test you can use the 'on-screen' calculator. You answer questions using the mouse and the keyboard and you can move between questions by using the 'next' and 'previous' buttons. You can return to questions either by using the 'flag' button and then the 'review' button or by waiting until the end of the test when you will have the option of reviewing all the questions – provided there is time.

Section 4.4 provides guidance, examples and questions on *solving* written arithmetic problems. Your ability to use general everyday arithmetic is assessed. For example, in working correctly with: time; money; ratio and proportion; fractions; decimals and percentages; distance and area; conversions between currencies; and simple formulae and averages, including mean, median, mode and range.

Section 4.5 provides guidance, examples and questions on *interpreting* and using written data. Your ability to identify trends correctly, to make comparisons and draw conclusions, and interpret charts and tables correctly is assessed.

Time for the test
The mental test will take about 12 minutes, the on-screen test will take about 36 minutes.

The contexts for the questions

One of the aims of the numeracy skills test is to ensure that teachers have the skills and understanding necessary to analyse the sort of data that is now in schools. Consequently most questions will be set within contexts such as:

- national test data;
- target setting and school improvement data;
- pupil progress and attainment over time;
- special educational needs (SEN);
- GCSE subject choices and results.

Hints and advice

The mental arithmetic, audio section
Each mental arithmetic question is heard twice. After the first reading an answer box appears on the screen. You will have a short time – 18 seconds – to work out the answer and type it into the answer box, after which the next question will automatically appear. As mentioned earlier, you cannot move forwards or backwards between questions. At the start of the test you will hear a practice question.

- Concentrate the first time the question is read, and note down the key numbers. For example, a question could be: 'In a class of 30 pupils, 24 are boys. What fraction are girls?'. You should jot down 30 and 24. The second time the question is heard, concentrate on what to do with those numbers (for example, $30 - 24 = 6$ (so there are 6 girls) then $\frac{6}{30} = \frac{1}{5}$).
- Start to work out the answer as soon as you have the information. You may be able to do this while you hear the second reading of the question.
- If you cannot answer a question don't worry or panic – enter a likely answer, then forget it. Remember, you don't need to get every single question right.

- Note that you don't have to worry about units, i.e. £ or € or cm, for example. The units will appear in the answer box.
- Listen carefully to what the question requires in the answer. For example, a question could ask for a time 'using the 24-hour clock', or an answer 'to the nearest whole number', or 'to two decimal places'. (There are notes on this in Section 4.4)
- Fractions need to be entered in the lowest terms. For example, 6/8 should be entered as 3/4 and 7/28 should be entered as 1/4.
- Practise using mental strategies. For example, purchasing five books that cost £5.99 can be worked out by multiplying 5 x £6 (£30) and subtracting 5 x lp (5p) to give the answer of £29.95.
- Remember the link between fractions and percentages – see page 120.

The on-screen questions

- Try not to spend more than two minutes on any one question and keep an eye on the time remaining. If you think you are exceeding the time then move on – you can always return to any you still need to complete at the end of the test and insert an answer. Try not to leave any answers blank at the end of the test.
- Read each question carefully. For example, a question may ask for the percentage of pupils who achieved grade 4 and above. Don't just look at those who gained grade 4; the question included the words 'and above', so you need to include those who achieved 'above', i.e. achieved grade 5, grade 6, and so on.
- Check that you are giving the correct information in the answer. A table may give you details of the number of marks a pupil achieved but the question may be asking for a percentage score.

The on-screen calculator

When the mental arithmetic section of the test is finished, a basic four-function calculator will be available on the screen for you to use for the rest of the test. No other calculators can be used. You can move the calculator around the screen using the mouse. The on-screen calculator works through the mouse and through the number pad on the keyboard. If you wish to use the number pad you must ensure that the number lock key 'Num Lock' is activated.

Notes on using the on-screen calculator

- To cancel an operation, press ⌷CE⌷.
- Always use the 'clear' button ⌷C⌷ on the calculator before beginning a new calculation.
- Always check the display of the calculator to make sure that the number shown is what you wanted.
- Check calculations and make sure that your final answer makes sense in the context of the question. For example, the number of pupils gaining 60% in a test will not be greater than the size of the cohort or group.

Other hints

1. Rounding up and down

- Make sure that any instructions to round an answer up or down are followed – or the answer will be marked as incorrect.
- Use the context to make sure whether a decimal answer should be rounded up or down. For example, an answer of 16.4 lessons for a particular activity is clearly not appropriate and the answer would need to be rounded up to 17 lessons.

- Questions may specify that the answer should be rounded to the nearest whole number or be rounded to two decimal places. See the notes at the start of Section 4.4.
- When carrying out calculations relating to money, the answer shown on the calculator display will need to be rounded to the nearest penny (unless otherwise indicated). Hence, if calculating in pounds, round to two decimal places to show the number of pence. If 10.173 is the answer in pounds on the calculator display, rounding to the nearest penny gives £10.17.

2. Answering multi-stage questions

The calculator provided is not a scientific calculator and therefore care needs to be taken with 'mixed operations' (i.e. calculations using several function keys). It is important that the function keys are pressed in the appropriate order for the calculation. It may also be useful to note down answers to particular stages of the calculation.

It is important to remember to carry out the calculation required by the question in the following order: any calculation within brackets followed by division/multiplication followed by addition and/or subtraction. Thus, the answer to the calculation $2 + 3 \times 4$ is 14 and not 20; the answer to $\frac{18}{3+6}$ is $\frac{18}{9} = 2$; and the answer to $\frac{18}{3} + 6 = 6 + 6 = 12$. See the notes at the start of Section 4.4.

3. Dealing with fractions

Although fractions will appear in the usual format within a question (for example, $\frac{3}{4}$), to enter a fraction in an answer, use the 'forward slash' key (for example, 'one-half' would be entered as 1/2). To use the on-screen calculator to calculate with fractions then it is probably easier to deal with the fraction first, converting it into a decimal, and then multiply by this decimal. For example, to calculate $\frac{5}{8}$ of 320, first enter $5/8 = 0.625$. Multiply 0.625 by 320, obtaining 200 as the answer.

How to use this chapter

This chapter is divided into five sections, following this introduction.

Section 4.2: this very short section has been included to remind you of the basic arithmetic processes. The majority of you will be able to miss this unit out, but some may welcome a chance to revise fractions, decimals, percentages, etc.

Sections 4.3 to 4.5: these cover the three 'content' areas (see above), one area per section.

Section 4.6: this contains answers and key points for all the questions in the main section.

In each section, the additional required knowledge, language and vocabulary are explained, and worked examples of the type of questions to be faced are provided, together with the practice questions. The answers for these questions are given in Section 4.6, together with further advice and guidance on solutions.

Revision checklists
The following charts show in detail the coverage of the three main sections and the practice tests. You can use the checklists in your revision to make sure that you have covered all the key content areas.

Revision checklist for Section 4.3: Mental arithmetic

Syllabus Reference	Content	Question
1a	Time – varied contexts	1, 7, 18, 21, 34, 36, 40, 42
1b	Amounts of money–varied contexts	10, 12, 38, 44
1c/d/e	lc Proportion – answer as a fraction ld Proportion – answer as a percentage le Proportion – answer as a decimal	37 22
1f	Fractions	16, 29
1g	Decimals	25, 32, 39
1h	Percentages – varied contexts	2, 4, 9, 11, 13, 19, 20, 24, 26, 28, 35, 37, 41, 43
1i/j/k	li Measurements–distance lj Measurements – area lk Measurements – other	23 45 40
1l/m/n/o/p/q	ll Conversions – from one currency to another	36
	lm Conversions – from fractions to decimals	15
	ln Conversions – from decimals to fractions	
	lo Conversions – from percentages to fractions	31
	lp Conversions – from fractions to percentages	30, 33
	lq Conversions – other	6
1r	Combination of one or more of addition, subtraction, multiplication, division (may involve amounts of money or whole numbers)	3, 5, 8, 14, 17,27

Revision checklist for Section 4.4: Solving written arithmetic problems.

(Note: Only the main references are used; many questions will cover more than one reference.)

Syllabus Reference	Content	Question
3a	Time – varied contexts	7, 17, 29, 31, 33, 37
3b	Amounts of money	2, 32, 57, 60
3c, d, e, f	3c Proportion – answer as a fraction	14
	3d Proportion – answer as a percentage	14
	3e Proportion – answer as a decimal	13, 14, 35
	3f Ratios	3
3g	Percentages – varied contexts	4, 5, 6, 8, 12, 13, 18, 24, 27, 37, 41, 42, 44, 47, 53, 59, 62
3h	Fractions	9, 10, 19, 24, 54, 57
3i	Decimals	

Syllabus Reference	Content	Question
3j, k, l, m, n	3j Measurements – distance	21, 26, 28, 30, 35, 36
	3k Measurements – area	22
	3l Conversions – from one currency to another	
	3m Conversions – from fractions to decimals or vice versa	
	3n Conversions – other	15, 16, 20, 25, 38, 39, 48, 61
3o, p, q, r, s	3o Averages – mean	1, 11, 23, 34, 45, 58
	3p Averages – median	23, 45
	3q Averages – mode	1
	3r Range	11, 35, 45
	3s Averages – combination	1, 23
3t	Given formulae	40, 43, 46, 49, 50, 51, 52, 55, 56

Revision checklist for Section 4.5: Interpreting and using written data

(Note: Only the main references are used; many questions will cover more than one reference.)

Syllabus Reference	Content	Question
2a	Identify trends over time	9, 13, 19, 21
2b	Make comparisons in order to draw conclusions	2, 5, 10, 11, 12, 14, 17, 23, 24
2c	Interpret and use information	1, 3, 4, 6, 7, 8, 15, 16, 18, 20, 22
3o	Averages	

4.2 Key knowledge

Fractions, decimals and percentages

Essentially fractions, decimals and percentages are the same things. They are all ways of writing numbers.

In the following explanations you will need to remember that a factor is a number that will divide into another number. For example, 3 is a factor of 6; 2 is a factor of 10.

Fractions

(i) A simple fraction, eg $\frac{3}{5}$, has a numerator (the top number) and a denominator (the bottom number). Both the numerator and the denominator will be whole numbers.

(ii) $\frac{3}{5}$ means 3 parts out of 5, or 3 divided by 5, or 3 shared by 5 or 3 lots of a fifth, or a fifth of 3. They all equal $3 \div 5$, which is 0.6. Why? Think about a short division calculation:

$$5 \overline{)3.^{3}0} \quad \frac{0.6}{}$$

5 into 3 doesn't go (goes 'o' times); there is a "carry over" (a remainder) of 3. 5 into 30 goes 6. So the answer is 0.6

But of course with a calculator the calculation is easy and straightforward. $3 \div 5 = 0.6$

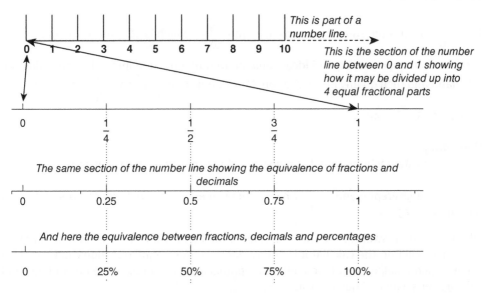

(iii) Equivalent fractions are formed by multiplying (or dividing) both the numerator and the denominator of a given fraction by the same number. For example:

$\frac{3}{5} = \frac{6}{10}$ multiplying the numerator and denominator by 2

$\frac{9}{15} = \frac{3}{5}$ dividing the numerator and denominator by 3 which is a common factor. This is called cancelling. If an answer requires a fraction in its simplest form, you may need to cancel. This is shown in the following question:

" in a year group of 72 children, 30 are boys. What fraction of the year group are boys? Give your answer in its lowest terms."

The fraction $\frac{boys}{total} =$

$\frac{30}{72}$ $\xrightarrow{\text{dividing the numerator and denominator by 2 which is a common factor}}$ $\frac{15}{36}$ $\xrightarrow{\text{dividing the numerator and denominator by 3 which is a common factor}}$ $\frac{5}{12}$

There is no common factor of 5 and 12 so this is the answer given in its lowest terms.

(iv) In the mental test when answering questions asking you to find a fraction of a quantity you will need to do some multiplication and division. For example:

find $\frac{3}{5}$ of 225. Solution: $\frac{1}{5}$ of 225 = 45 (why? Divide 225 by 5 ..... $5\overline{)225}$)

so $\frac{3}{5} = 3 \times 45 = 135$

Remember to round answers if necessary and appropriate. For example money will only have 2 decimal places and a number of people will always be a whole number.

Decimals
Decimals are fractions with denominators which are multiples of 10 or 100 or 1000 or ....

Thus $\frac{4}{10}$ which is the same as $4 \div 10 = 0.4$, and $\frac{56}{1000}$ which is $56 \div 1000 = 0.056$.

For on-screen questions a good idea would be to turn a fraction into a decimal using the calculator and then do any multiplication, for example find $\frac{4}{5}$ of £48. $\frac{4}{5} = 0.8$. and

$0.8 \times £48 = £38.40$

Percentages

Percentages are fractions with denominators of 100 (per cent means per 100).

For example 5% represents $\frac{5}{100}$ which is the same as 0.05. 75% represents $\frac{75}{100}$, and this equals 0.75.

When you are answering the on-screen questions you will have access to a simple 4 function calculator. The calculator is not available for the mental questions and therefore you may find it helpful to adopt a different approach, based for example on doubling and halving. Thus a mental question such as:

"find 35% of £200" would be tackled by

- finding 10% and multiplying by 3 to give 30%,
- then halving the 10% value to find 5%
- then adding the two answers together.

Thus 10% of £200 = £20. Therefore 30% = £60 and 5% = £10.

Therefore 35% = £60 + £10 = £70.

To change a fraction into a percentage first change it into a decimal and then multiply by 100. For example $\frac{3}{8} = 0.375 = 37.5\%$.

Here are some common fractions, decimals and percentages.

You should learn these.

1%	$\frac{1}{100}$	0.01	(divide by 100)
5%	$\frac{1}{20}$	0.05	(divide by 20)
10%	$\frac{1}{10}$	0.1	(divide by 10)
$12\frac{1}{2}\%$	$\frac{1}{8}$	0.125	(divide by 8)
20%	$\frac{1}{5}$	0.2	(divide by 5)
25%	$\frac{1}{4}$	0.25	(divide by 4)
50%	$\frac{1}{2}$	0.5	(divide by 2)
75%	$\frac{3}{4}$	0.75	(divide by 4, multiply by 3)

1   Simplify these fractions, writing them in their lowest terms

   (a) $\dfrac{24}{36}$ (b) $\dfrac{18}{30}$ (c) $\dfrac{75}{100}$ (d) $\dfrac{27}{45}$

2   Write these percentages as decimals

   (a) 15%   (b) 36%   (c) 65%   (d) 2%

3   Work out, without using a calculator

   (a) 28×2.5 (b) 3×3.45 (c) 0.9×180 (d) 1.5×15

4   Calculate, without using a calculator

   (a) 40% of 240   (b) 75% of 120   (c) 25% of 36   (d) 80% of 60

5   Find:

   (a) $\dfrac{3}{4}$ of 60   (b) $\dfrac{5}{8}$ of 64   (c) $\dfrac{2}{5}$ of 120   (d) $\dfrac{3}{8}$ of 560

6   Write these fractions as percentages

   (a) $\dfrac{3}{8}$ (b) $\dfrac{4}{5}$ (c) $\dfrac{11}{25}$ (d) $\dfrac{28}{35}$

7   Write these percentages as fractions in their lowest terms

   (a) 85%   (b) 30%   (c) 64%   (d) 6%

Mean, median, mode and range

The *mean* is the average most people give if asked for an average – the mean is found by adding up all the values in the list and dividing this total by the number of values.

The *median* is the middle value when all the values in the list are put in size order. If there are two 'middle' values the median is the mean of these two.

The *mode* is the most common value.

The *range* is the difference between the highest value and the lowest value.

Example

This example should illustrate each of the four calculations.

The children in Class 6 gained the following marks in a test:

Boys		45	46	48	60	42	53	47	51
		54	54	49	48	47	53	48	45
Girls		45	47	47	55	46	53	54	63
		48	50	46	51	48	48		

Work out the mean, median, mode and range for the boys and girls and compare the distributions of the marks.

The calculation for the boys:

$$Mean: \frac{42+45+45+46+47+47+48+48+48+49+51+53+53+54+54+60}{16}$$

= 49 (to the nearest whole number)

Median: there are 16 values, so the median is midway between the 8th and 9th values

$$= \frac{48+48}{2} = 48$$

The *mode* is 48.

The *range* is 60 − 42 = 18.

4.3 Mental arithmetic

Notes

The mathematics required in this part of the test should usually be straightforward. The content and skills likely to be tested are listed in the Introduction (see page 113). Look back at this to remind yourself.

> **Key point**
> When you are taking the test, listen for, and jot down, numbers that may give short-cuts or ease the calculations, such as those that allow doubling and halving. For example, multiply by 100 then divide by 2 if you need to multiply by 50, or multiply by 100 and divide by 4 if you are multiplying by 25. To calculate percentages, first find 10% by dividing by 10 then double for 20% or divide by 2 for 5% and so on. Look back at the hints in the Introduction.

Remember
- Calculators are not allowed.
- Questions will be read out twice. When answering the questions in this section, ask someone to read each question out to you and then, without a pause, read out the question again.
- There should then be a pause to allow you to record the answer before the next question is read out. The pause should be 18 seconds long.

Hint

You might find it helpful to ask someone to read out these practice questions. They will need to read them out at a sensible speed, as if they were reading a story to children. Remind them that each question should be read out twice and that they should then pause for 18 seconds, before reading out the next question. Numbers in these questions are in words, rather than using digits, to emphasise that they are spoken.

Questions

1. As part of a two and a quarter hour tennis training session, pupils received specialist coaching for one hour and twenty minutes. How many minutes of the training session remained?

2. A test has forty questions, each worth one mark. The pass mark was seventy per cent. How many questions had to be answered correctly to pass the test?

3. Dining tables seat six children. How many tables are needed to seat one hundred children?

4. Three classes of twenty-eight pupils took the end of Key Stage two mathematics test. Sixty-three pupils gained a scaled score of one hundred. What percentage is this?

5. A coach holds fifty-two passengers. How many coaches will be needed for a school party of four hundred and fifty people?

6. Eight kilometres is about five miles. About how many kilometres is thirty miles?

7. The journey from school to a sports centre took thirty-five minutes each way. The pupils spent two hours at the sports centre. They left school at oh-nine-thirty. At what time did they return?

8. It is possible to seat forty people in a row across the hall. How many rows are needed to seat four hundred and thirty-two people?

9. Pupils spent twenty-five hours in lessons each week. Four hours per week were allocated to science. What percentage of the lesson time per week was spent on the other subjects?

10. The total cost of a school's play is two hundred and eighty-five pounds. Ninety-four adults pay two pounds fifty each to watch the play. How much profit did the school make?

11. In a mock GCSE examination, eighty per cent of the pupils in class A achieved grade C and above. In class B twenty-two out of twenty-five pupils reached the same standard. What was the difference between the two classes in the percentage of pupils reaching grade C and above?

12. Two hundred pupils correctly completed a sponsored spell of fifty words. Each pupil was sponsored at five pence per word. How much money did the pupils raise in total?

Questions

13. A pupil scores forty-two marks out of a possible seventy in a class test. What percentage score is this?

14. There are one hundred and twenty pupils in a year group. Each has to take home two notices. Paper costs three pence per copy. How much will the notices cost?

15. What is seven and a half per cent as a decimal?

16. In a class of thirty-five pupils, four out of seven are boys. How many girls are there in the class?

17. In a school there are five classes of twenty-five pupils and five classes of twenty-eight pupils. How many pupils are there in the school?

18. A school has four hours and twenty-five minutes class contact time per day. What is the weekly contact time (assume a five-day week)?

19. In part one of an examination a pupil scored eighteen marks out of a possible twenty-five marks, in part two he scored sixteen marks out of a possible twenty-five marks. What was his final score for the examination? Give your answer as a percentage.

20. In a year group of one hundred and twenty pupils, eighty per cent achieved a level four or a level five in Key Stage two English. Sixty pupils achieved a level five. How many pupils achieved a level four?

21. A teacher wants to record a film on a three-hour video tape which starts at eleven fifty-five p.m. and ends at one forty-five a.m. the following day. How much time will there be left on the tape?

22. In a year group of one hundred and forty-four pupils fifty-four pupils travel to school on school buses. What proportion of the year group does not travel on school buses? Give your answer as a decimal.

23. A space two point five metres by two point five metres is to be used for a flower bed. What is this area in square metres?

24. In a class of thirty pupils, sixty per cent of the pupils are girls. How many boys are there in the class?

25. In a Year Eleven tutor group of thirty pupils, the proportion who planned to stay on into Year Twelve was nought point seven. How many pupils did not plan to stay on into year twelve?

26. Twenty per cent of the pupils in a school with three hundred and fifteen pupils have free school meals. How many pupils is this?

Questions

27. A teacher prepares an activity for a group of thirty-one pupils. The activity requires the pupils to work in groups of no more than four. Each group will need two rulers. What is the maximum number of rulers required?

28. A pupil scores fourteen out of a possible twenty-five in a test. What is this as a percentage?

29. Three-fifths of a class of thirty-five pupils are boys. How many are girls?

30. In an end-of-year test, nineteen pupils out of a class of twenty-five pupils gained half marks or more. What percentage of pupils gained less than half marks?

31. What is twelve and one half per cent as a decimal?

32. What is four point zero five six multiplied by one hundred?

33. Two-fifths of pupils starting secondary school in September did not speak English as their first language. What percentage of the pupils did speak English as their first language?

34. A bus journey starts at zero eight fifty-five. It lasts for forty minutes. At what time does it finish? Give your answer using the twenty-four hour clock system.

35. Twenty per cent of the pupils in Year Ten play hockey. Twenty-five per cent play basketball. The rest play football. There are two hundred pupils in Year Ten. How many play football? 1

36. A school group stays in Germany for two nights. The cost of accommodation for each member of the group is fifty-five euros per night. The exchange rate is one pound equals one point one euros. What is the cost of the accommodation in pounds for each person?

37. Out of one hundred and forty-four pupils in Year Eleven, forty-eight do not continue in full-time education. What proportion of Year Eleven pupils does continue in full-time education? Give your answer as a fraction in its lowest terms.

38. A teacher travels from school to a training course. After the course is over she returns to school. The distance to the training venue is twenty-four miles and expenses are paid at a rate of forty pence per mile. How much will she receive?

39. A part-time teacher has a contract to work for nought point four of the full-time equivalent contract per week. A full-time week is five days. How many days per week would the teacher work?

40. For a practical task, a science teacher needs twenty-five millilitres of liquid for each pupil. There are twenty pupils in the class. How many millilitres of liquid are needed?

Questions

41. A class of twenty-four students takes GCSE French. The proportion of the class achieving grades A or A* is twelve and a half per cent. How many students achieve grades A or A*?

42. A primary school football match is scheduled to kick off at fifteen forty-five. Each half will last twenty-five minutes with a five-minute interval. What is the earliest time that the match will finish? Give your answer using the twenty-four hour clock.

43. The cost of the coach for a class history visit was two hundred and twenty-four pounds. The coach company announces that prices will increase by fifteen per cent next year. How much should the school expect to pay for the coach next year?

44. The pupils in a primary school take part in a charity skipping event. Five of the three hundred and sixty-five pupils are absent. The rest contribute one pound fifty each. What is the total amount the school raises for charity?

45. A vegetable bed in the school garden measures three metres by three metres. Pupils have to apply fertiliser at a rate of one hundred grams per square metre. What is the minimum amount of fertiliser, in kilograms, that the teacher should have available?

4.4 Solving written arithmetic problems

Notes

Many of the questions in the skills test will require you to be able to interpret charts, tables and graphs. These are usually straightforward but do make sure that you read the questions carefully and read the tables or graphs carefully so that you will be able to identify the correct information. These questions are so varied that it is difficult to give examples for all of them – practice makes perfect, though.

There are some questions for which you may wish to revise the mathematics.

Fractions and percentages
See the brief notes in Section 4.2 for the essential knowledge. If you have to calculate percentage increases (or decreases), the simplest method is: find the actual difference, divide by the original amount and then multiply by 100 to convert this fraction to a percentage.

Example

Last year 30 pupils gained a level 3 in the National Tests. This year 44 gained a level 3. Calculate the percentage increase.

Actual increase = 14.
Percentage increase = $\frac{14}{30}$ x 100 = 46.667%.
(But note the comment below on rounding.)

Rounding

Clearly this answer, 46.667%, is too accurate. It would be better written as 46.7% (written to one decimal place) or as 47% (to the nearest whole number). You need to be able to round answers to a given number of decimal places or to the nearest whole number (depending on what the question is demanding). The simple rule is that if the first digit that you wish to remove is 5 or more, then you add 1 to the last remaining digit in the answer. If the first digit is less than 5 then the digits are just removed.

Examples:

46.3	= 46	to the nearest whole number
0.345	= 0.35	to two decimal places
34.3478	= 34.348	to three decimal places
34.3478	= 34.35	to two decimal places
34.3478	= 34.3	to one decimal place
34.3478	= 34	to the nearest whole number

Ratio and proportion

These sorts of questions are best illustrated with examples:

Example

(a) Divide £60 between 3 people in the ratio 1:2:3.

The total number of 'parts' is $1 + 2 + 3 = 6$.

Therefore 1 part $= £60 \div 6 = £10$.

Therefore the money is shared as £10; £20; £30.

(b) Four times as many children in a class have school dinners as do not. If there are 30 children, how many have school dinners?

The ratio is 4:1 giving $4 + 1 = 5$ parts. Therefore 1 'part' $= 30 \div 5 = 6$. Therefore $4 \times 6 = 24$ children have school dinners.

Don't confuse ratio and proportion. Ratio is 'part to part' while proportion is 'part to whole' and is usually given as a fraction. If the question asked 'What proportion of children have school dinners?' the answer would be $\frac{24}{30} = \frac{4}{5}$.

Notes on measures

You need to know and be able to change between the main metric units of measurement. For example:

Length   1 kilometre = 1000 metres
1 metre = 100 centimetres or 1000 millimetres
1 centimetre = 10 millimetres

Mass   1 kilogram = 1000 grams
             1 tonne = 1000 kilograms

Capacity 1 litre = 1000 millilitres = 100 centilitres

Notes on algebra

Generally a formula will be given to you, either in words or letters, and you will need to substitute numbers into that formula and arrive at an answer through what will be essentially an arithmetic rather than algebraic process. Remember the rules that tell you the order in which you should work through calculations.

- **Brackets should be evaluated first.**
- **Then work out the multiplications and divisions.**
- **Finally work out the additions and subtractions.**

Thus: (i) $2 \times 3 + 4 = 6 + 4 = 10$, but $2 + 3 \times 4 = 14$ (i.e. $2 + 12$) not 20

(ii) $\dfrac{6+4}{2} = \dfrac{10}{2} = 5$ not $3 + 4 = 7$

Here do not divide the 6 by 2 which would give $3 + 4 = 7$ or the 4 by 2 which would give $6 + 2 = 8$.

(iii) $2(3 + 6) = 2 \times 9 = 18$

Note that some of the questions that follow have several parts. In the actual test each 'part' would be a separate question, for example question 1 could be split into three different questions, one to find the mean, one to find the mode and one to find the range.

Questions

1. There were 30 pupils in a class. Their results in a test are summarised in the table below.

Mark out of 40	Number of pupils achieving mark
19	2
24	8
27	1
29	5
33	2
34	5
36	7

What are the mean, mode and range for these results?

Questions

2. A teacher was planning a school trip to Germany. Each pupil was to be allowed €100 spending money. At the time she planned the trip £1 was equivalent to €1.14. How much English money did each pupil need to exchange in order to receive €100?

3. Five times as many pupils in a school obtained a scaled score of 100 in the Key Stage 2 mathematics test as obtained a score of 101. No pupil scored less than 100. If a total of 32 pupils took the test and just 2 pupils scored more than 101, how many pupils scored 100?

4. Teachers in a mathematics department analysed the Key Stage 2 National Test results for mathematics from three feeder schools.

Scaled score	School A Number of pupils	School B Number of pupils	School C Number of pupils	Totals
98	5	3	4	12
99	6	8	8	22
100	16	18	15	49
101	6	3	8	17
Totals	33	32	35	

Which school had the greatest percentage of pupils with a score of 100 and above?

5. The national percentage of pupils with SEN (including statements) is about 18%. A school of 250 pupils has 35 children on the SEN register. How many children is this below the national average?

6. A secondary school analysed its GCSE results for French for the period 2013–16. The table shows the number of pupils at each grade.

French	Grade A	Grade B	Grade C	Grade D or lower
2016	19	15	7	1
2015	14	18	3	
2014	23	21	4	
2013	21	16	5	6

Which of the following statements is correct?

(a) The percentage of pupils gaining grade A or grade B in 2013 was greater than in 2016.

(b) The percentage of pupils who failed to gain a grade A was greater in 2015 than in 2014.

(c) The percentage of pupils gaining grade A in 2016 was approximately 5 percentage points higher than in 2015.

Questions

7. An end of year assessment for a class of 27 Year 10 pupils was planned to take 6 hours. As part of the assessment each pupil required access to a computer for 25% of the time. The school's ICT suite contained 30 computers and could be booked for a number of 40-minute sessions.

   How many computer sessions needed to be booked for the class?

8. A pupil achieved a mark of 58 out of 75 for practical work and 65 out of 125 on the written paper. The practical mark was worth 60% of the final mark and the written paper 40% of the final mark. The minimum mark required for each grade is shown below.

Grade	Minimum mark
A*	80%
A	65%
B	55%
C	45%
D	35%

   What was the grade achieved by this pupil?

9. A pupil obtained the following marks in three tests.

   In which test did the pupil do best?

Test 1	Test 2	Test 3
$\frac{45}{60}$	$\frac{28}{40}$	$\frac{23}{30}$

10. A school has a target that at least $\frac{2}{3}$ of the pupils in a class should have parents or carers coming to parents' evenings.

    A week before the Year 7 parents evening a deputy head compiled this table:

Class	Number in class	Number of pupils with parents/carers attending
7SW	25	15
7MP	27	17
7PH	31	23
7TS	32	20
7TM	29	24

    Which classes are meeting the school's target?

11. The scores for a group of pupils in a series of English tests are shown below:

Pupil	Test 1	Test 2	Test 3	Test 4	Test 5
A	19	13	15	17	11
B	6	9	5	10	15
C	13	14	11	13	14
D	18	12	20	12	18

Indicate all the true statements:

A   The highest mean score by a pupil is 16.

B   Pupil B has the greatest range of test scores.

C   All pupils scored more in Test 5 than in Test 1.

12. A teacher analysed the number of pupils in a school achieving level 4 and above in the end of Key Stage 2 English tests for 2012–15.

	Year			
	2012	2013	2014	2015
Pupils achieving level 4 and above	70	74	82	84
Pupils in year group	94	98	104	110

In each year the school was set a target of 75% of pupils to achieve a level 4 or above in the end of Key Stage 2 English tests.

(a) By how many percentage points did the school exceed its target in 2015? Give your answer to the nearest whole number.

(b) In which year was the target exceeded by the greatest margin?

13. A primary school teacher records the difference between the reading ages and actual ages of the 30 pupils in her class, grouping the results together. The table shows that, for example, there are 3 boys whose reading ages are more than 3 years and up to 6 years below their actual ages.

Difference between reading age and actual age in months, d (reading age – actual age)	Number of pupils	
	Boys	Girls
$-9 < d \le -15$	1	1
$-6 < d \le -9$	3	1
$-3 < d \le -6$	3	
$0 < d \le -3$	2	2

Questions

Difference between reading age and actual age in months, d (reading age – actual age)	Number of pupils	
	Boys	Girls
0		2
$0 < d \leq +3$	3	1
$+3 < d \leq +6$	1	3
$+6 < d \leq +9$	1	3
$+9 < d \leq +15$	1	2

Indicate all the true statements:

A   More boys than girls have reading ages below their actual ages.

B   The proportion of girls with a reading age greater than their actual age is 0.6

C   3 pupils have a reading age of 1 year or more above their actual age.

14. Four schools had the following proportion of pupils with SEN.

School	Proportion
P	$\dfrac{2}{9}$
Q	0.17
R	57 out of 300
S	18%

Which school had the lowest proportion of pupils with SEN?

A School P   B School Q   C School R   D School S

15. This table shows the marks gained by a group of pupils in Year 3 in a mathematics test.

Pupil	Marks	Pupil	Marks
A	36	K	56
B	62	L	54
C	64	M	32
D	42	N	35
E	46	O	67
F	50	P	58
G	63	Q	63
H	68	R	60
I	39	S	62
J	61	T	58

The school will use the results to predict their levels for mathematics at the end of Year 6, and will target those pupils who, it is predicted, will achieve scaled scores of less than 100 in the Year 6 tests.

This is the conversion chart the school uses to change marks to expected scaled scores:

Mark range	<40	40 – 59	60 – 64	65 and over
Expected scaled score	85 – 94	95 – 99	100	101 – 120

How many pupils will be targeted?

16. A school has analysed the results of its students at GCSE and A level for several years and from these produced a graph which it uses to predict the average A level points score for a given average points score at GCSE.

Use the graph below to predict the points score at A level if the GCSE points score were 6.

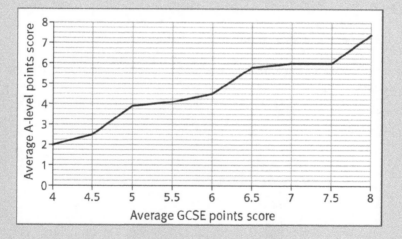

17. A junior school has a weekly lesson time of 23.5 hours. Curriculum analysis gives the following amount of time to the core subjects:

English:	6 hours 30 mins
Mathematics:	5 hours
Science:	1 hour 30 mins

Calculate the percentage of curriculum time given to English. Give your answer to the nearest per cent.

Questions

18. A support teacher assessed the reading ages of a group of 10 Year 8 pupils with SEN.

	Actual age		Reading age	
Pupil	Years	Months	Years	Months
A	12	07	10	08
B	12	01	11	09
C	12	03	9	07
D	12	03	13	06
E	12	01	10	02
F	12	11	12	00
G	12	06	8	04
H	12	07	10	00
I	12	06	11	08
J	12	02	10	10

What percentage of the 10 pupils had a reading age of at least 1 year 6 months below the actual age?

19. A teacher analysed pupils' performance at the end of Year 5 in 2015.

Pupils judged to have achieved level 3 and below were targeted for extra support.

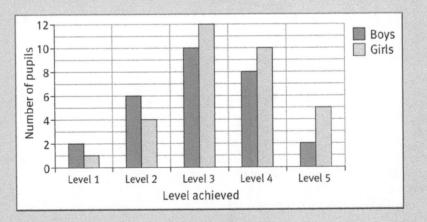

What fraction of the pupils needed extra support?

20. A plastic drinking cup has a capacity of 100ml.

How many cups could be filled from a 1.5 litre carton of juice?

Questions

21. A teacher recorded the number of laps of a rectangular field walked by pupils in Years 5 and 6 in a school's annual walk for charity.

Year group	Number of pupils	Number of laps
5	65	8
6	94	10

The rectangular field measured 200 metres by 150 metres.

The teacher calculated the total distance covered.

Which of the following shows the total distance in kilometres?

A 1022   B 1460   C 10220   D 111.3

22. A primary teacher required each pupil to have a piece of card measuring 20cm by 45cm for a lesson. Large sheets of card measured 60cm by 50cm. What was the minimum number of large sheets of card required for a class of 28 pupils?

23. In a review of the test performance of 3 pupils a teacher prepares a table of their marks in a series of class tests.

Percentage marks in each test

Pupil	Test 1	Test 2	Test 3	Test 4	Test 5	Mean mark	Median mark
A	39	50	34	32	35	38	Place here
B	37	48	32	28	30	35	32
C	36	47	34	33	45	Place here	34

| 32 | | 35 | | 38 | | 39 | |

What are the correct values of (a) the median and (b) the mean to be placed in the correct boxes?

24. This table shows the GCSE grades in design and technology achieved by a school's Year 11 pupils for the period 2013 to 2016.

Grade	A*	A	B	C	D	E	F/G	Total number of students
2013	1	2	2	11	5	6	1	28
2014	6	5	9	13	1	0	0	34
2015	4	7	9	16	4	0	0	40
2016	5	6	8	10	4	2	1	36

Questions

Which of the following statements is correct?

A   2014 had the highest percentage of grades A and A*.

B   2015 had the lowest percentage of grade C.

C   Less than $\frac{1}{4}$ of pupils gained a grade B in any year.

25. Using the relationship 5 miles = 8km, convert:

    (a) 120 miles into kilometres;

    (b) 50km into miles.

    (Give your answers to the nearest whole number in each case.)

26. A ream of photocopier paper (500 sheets) is approximately 5cm thick. What is the approximate thickness of 1 sheet of paper? Give your answer in millimetres.

27. A teacher organised revision classes for pupils who achieved grades C and D in mock examinations and used the following table to assess the number of pupils who might benefit from attending the classes.

Grade	Boys	Girls	Total
A*	3	5	8
A	4	3	7
B	6	8	14
C	7	4	11
D	4	5	9
E	3	3	6
F	2	2	4
G	1	0	1

What percentage of the pupils would benefit from attending the classes?

Give your answer to the nearest whole number.

28. A piece of fabric measuring 32cm by 15cm was required for each pupil in a Year 8 design and technology lesson. What was the minimum length of 120cm wide fabric required for 29 pupils?

29. A school trip is organised from Derby to London – approximately 120 miles. A teacher makes the following assumptions.

    (a) The pupils will need a 30-minute break during the journey.

    (b) The coach will be able to average 40 miles an hour, allowing for roadworks and traffic.

    (c) The coach is due in London at 9 a.m.

    What would be the latest time for the coach to leave Derby?

30. A teacher organised a hike for a group of pupils during a school's activity week. The route was measured on a 1:50 000 scale map and the distances on the map for each stage of the hike were listed on the chart below.

Stage of hike		Distance on map (cm)
1.	Start to Stop A	14.3
2.	Stop A to Stop B	8.7
3.	Stop B to Stop C	9.3

    What was the total distance travelled on the hike?

    Give your answer to the nearest kilometre.

31. The following table shows the time for 4 children swimming in a relay race.

1st length	John	95.6 seconds
2nd length	Karen	87.3 seconds
3rd length	Julie	91.3 seconds
4th length	Robert	89.4 seconds

    What was the total time, in minutes and seconds, that they took?

32. A teacher completed the following expenses claim form after attending a training course.

Travelling From	To	Miles	Expenses
School and return	Training centre to school	238	Place here
Other expenses	Car parking		£7.50
	Evening meal		£10.50
		Total claim	Place here

    The mileage rates were:

    30p per mile for the first 100 miles

    26p per mile for the remainder.

    Complete the claim form by placing the correct values in the expenses column.

    | £40.88 | £65.88 | £71.38 | £73.88 | £83.88 | £87.00 | £89.40 |

33. A classroom assistant works from 9:00 a.m. until 12 noon for 4 days per week in a primary school and has a 15 minute break from 10:30 until 10:45. She provides learning support for pupils – each pupil receiving a continuous 20 minute session. How many pupils can she support each week?

34. The mean height of 20 girls in Year 7 is 1.51m. Another girl who is 1.6m joins the class. Calculate the new mean height.

Questions

35. A primary school teacher produces a table showing the differences between the reading age and the actual age for two tests for a group of 16 pupils.

Reading age minus actual age (months)

Test 1	Test 2
−10	−9
−9	−8
−7	−7
−7	−6
−5	−2
−2	0
0	0
0	2
3	4
3	3
3	6
6	7
7	8
9	9
9	10
10	10

(a) Which test had the greatest range in the values of 'reading age – actual age'?

(b) What proportion of pupils made no progress? Give your answer to one decimal place.

36. Equipment for a school is delivered in boxes 15cm deep. The boxes are to be stacked in a cupboard which is 1.24m high. How many layers of boxes will fit into the cupboard?

37. To inform planning a head of science produced a pie chart showing the subject choices made by 150 pupils entering the sixth form. How many more pupils chose to study maths than chose to study chemistry?

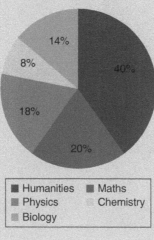

Sixth Form Choices

14%
8%
40%
18%
20%

■ Humanities ■ Maths
■ Physics   Chemistry
■ Biology

38. A teacher planned a school trip from Calais to a study centre. The distance from Calais to the centre is 400km. The coach is expected to travel at an average speed of 50 miles per hour, including time for breaks. The coach is due to leave Calais at 06:20. What time should it arrive at the study centre?

    Use the conversion rate of $1km = \frac{5}{8}mile$.

    Give your answer using the 24-hour clock.

39. The raw scores in a GCSE examination are converted to uniform marks (UMS) by using a graph, part of which is shown below.

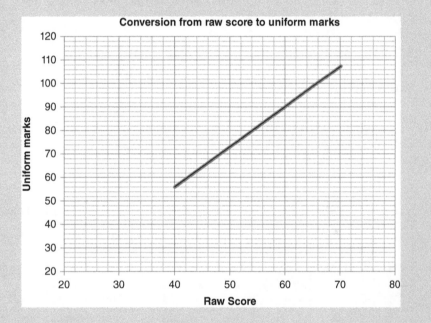

Uniform marks are then converted to grades using the following table of grade boundary marks:

Grade	A*	A	B	C	D	E	F
UMS	80	70	60	50	40	30	20

A student achieves a raw score of 52.

Select the grade that the student is awarded.

(a) A

(b) B

(c) C

Questions

The values for the graph are:

40	56
45	64.5
50	73
55	81.5
60	90
65	98.5
70	107

40. Moderators sample the coursework marked by teachers in school. A moderator will select a sample from a school according to the guidelines and rules. One rule that fixes the size of the sample to be selected is:

Size (s) = $10+\frac{n}{10}$ where n is the number of candidates in a school.

What would be the sample size if there were 150 candidates?

41. A teacher prepared tables to show the relationship between GCSE English Language grades and GCSE Mathematics and French grades.

	GCSE Grade	GCSE Mathematics						GCSE French					
		A*-A	B-C	D-E	F-G	U-X	Total	A*-A	B-C	D-E	F-G	U-X	Total
GCSE English language	A*-A	7	23	8			38	10	6				16
	B-C	5	40	10	2		57	10	16	1			27
	D-E		9	6	7	3	25		17	14	1	1	33
	F-G								1	1	2		4
	U-X												
	Total	12	72	24	9	3	120	20	40	16	3	1	80

Indicate all the true statements:

A The grade A*–C pass rate for GCSE French was 5 percentage points higher than the A*–C pass rate for mathematics.

B Of the pupils taking GCSE mathematics, more than half achieved grade C or above in GCSE English language.

C Of the pupils taking GCSE French, one third did not achieve grade C or above.

42. As part of a target-setting programme a teacher compared the marks for 10 pupils in each of 2 tests.

Questions

Pupils' marks out of 120

Pupil	Test 1	Test 2
A	70	66
B	61	68
C	64	63
D	56	41
E	70	78
F	60	59
G	64	77
H	72	80
I	39	44
J	62	57

Write down the letters for those pupils who scored at least 5 percentage points more in test 2 than test 1.

Note: In the actual test this question would be expressed as 'Indicate by clicking anywhere on the rows which pupils scored at least 5 percentage points more in test 2 than test 1'.

43. A pupil achieved the following scores in Tests A, B and C.

Test	A	B	C
Actual mark	70	60	7

The pupil's weighted score was calculated using the following formula:

$$\text{Weighted score} = \frac{(A \times 60)}{100} + \frac{(B \times 30)}{80} + C$$

What was the pupil's weighted score?

Give your answer to the nearest whole number.

44. A teacher used a spreadsheet to calculate pupils' marks in a mock GCSE exam made up of two papers. Paper 1 was worth 25% of the total achieved and Paper 2 was worth 75% of the total achieved.

This table shows the first four entries in the spreadsheet.

	Paper 1 Mark out of 30	(25%) Weighted mark	Paper 2 Mark out of 120	(75%) Weighted mark	Final weighted mark
Pupil A	24	20	80	50	70
Pupil B	20	16.7	68	42.5	59.2
Pupil C	8	6.7	59	36.9	43.6
Pupil D	20	16.7	74	46.3	63

Pupil E scored 18 on Paper 1 and 64 on Paper 2.

What was the final weighted mark for Pupil E?

Questions

45. The table below shows the percentage test results for a group of pupils.

Pupil	Test 1	Test 2	Test 3	Test 4	Test 5	Test 6	Test 7	Test 8
A	92	85	87	82	78	26	92	95
B	53	70	72	38	15	27	83	73
C	61	77	69	68	60	30	90	77
D	95	100	93	30	92	30	100	70
E	72	49	47	42	46	82	72	92
F	58	78	38	46	34	58	98	78

Indicate all the true statements.

A   The greatest range of % marks achieved was in test 2.

B   Pupil C achieved a mean mark of 66.5%.

C   The median mark for test 6 was 30.

46. A single mark for a GCSE examination is calculated from three components using the following formula:

Final mark = Component A × 0.6 + Component B × 0.3 + Component C × 0.1

A candidate obtained the following marks.

Component A   64
Component B   36
Component C   40

What was this candidate's final mark? Give your answer to the nearest whole number.

47. A pupil submitted two GCSE coursework tasks, Task A and Task B. Task A carried a weighting of 60% and Task B a weighting of 40%. Each task was marked out of 100.

The pupil scored 80 marks in Task A.

What would be the minimum mark score required by the pupil in Task B to achieve an overall mark across the two tasks of 60%?

48. A reading test consists of 4 parts. The scores are added together to provide a raw score. The table below converts raw scores into an age-standardised reading score.

	Age in years and months							
	6.05	6.06	6.07	6.08	6.09	6.10	6.11	7.00
Raw score	Age-standardised reading score							
16	97	97	96	96	96	96	96	96
17	98	98	98	98	97	97	97	97
18	99	99	99	99	99	98	98	98
19	101	100	100	100	100	100	99	99
20	102	102	101	101	101	101	101	101

A pupil whose age is 6 years and 10 months obtained scores of 2, 5, 4 and 7 from the four parts of the test.

What was the pupil's age standardised reading score?

49. A teacher calculated the speed in kilometres per hour of a pupil who completed a 6km cross-country race.

Use the formula: Distance = speed x time.

The pupil took 48 minutes.

What was the pupil's speed in kilometres per hour?

50. A readability test for worksheets, structured examination questions, etc. uses the formula:

$$\text{Reading level} = 5 + \left\{ 20 - \frac{X}{15} \right\}$$

where x = the average number of monosyllabic words per 150 words of writing.

Calculate the reading level for a paper where x = 20. Give your answer correct to two decimal places.

51. To help pupils set individual targets a teacher calculated predicted A-level points scores using the following formula:

$$\text{Predicted A-level points score} = \left(\frac{\text{total GCSE points score}}{\text{number of GCSEs}} \times 3.9 \right) - 17.5$$

GCSE grades were awarded the following points.

GCSE grade	A*	A	B	C
Points	8	7	6	5

Calculate the predicted A-level points score for a pupil who at GCSE gained 4 passes at grade C, 4 at grade B, 1 at grade A and 1 at grade A*.

52. A candidate's final mark in a GCSE examination is calculated from two components as follows:

Final mark = mark in component 1 x 0.6 + mark in component 2 x 0.4

A candidate needs a mark of 80 or more to be awarded a grade A*. If the mark awarded in component 2 was 70, what would be the lowest mark needed in component 1 to gain a grade A*?

Questions

53. A PGCE student looks at the Ofsted report for a secondary school which is advertising for a teacher in humanities.

Subject	Number of entries	% A*–A	% A*–C	% A*–G	% ungraded
History	80	35	85	98	2
Geography	60	20	65	95	5
Sociology	25	40	52	92	8
Psychology	28	35	55	100	0
English	166	42	80	99	1

Indicate all the true statements:

A 28 of the History students achieved an A* or an A grade.

B More students were ungraded in Sociology than in Geography.

C In English twice as many students gained an A*–C grade as gained an A*–A grade.

54. In the annual sports day at a school, pupils took part in a running race or in a field event or both. Pupils who took part in both were given an award. In Years 5 and 6 all 72 pupils took part in a running race or in a field event or both. $\frac{1}{2}$ took part in a running race and $\frac{3}{4}$ took part in a field event. How many pupils were given an award?

55. A school used the ALIS formula relating predicted A-level points scores to mean GCSE points scores for A-level mathematics pupils. The formula used was:

Predicted A-level points score = (mean GCSE points score x 2.24) – 7.35

What was the predicted A-level points score for a pupil with a mean GCSE points score of 7.55? Give your answer correct to one decimal place.

56. To inform a discussion on target setting, a head teacher compared the GCSE grades of pupils from schools in the same area.

	Percentage of pupils achieving 5 or more A*–C grades			
Year	School A	School B	School C	School D
2013	51	57	53	57
2014	53	60	54	62
2015	53	73	62	66
2016	56	81	66	69

Indicate all the true statements:

A   All the schools had an annual increase in the percentage of pupils achieving 5 or more A*–C grades over the four-year period.

B   Over the four-year period, school B had the greatest increase in the percentage of pupils achieving 5 or more A*–C grades.

C   In 2016, there was a 12 percentage points difference between the two highest achieving schools.

57. An English department organised a trip to the theatre for 35 pupils. The cost of the coach was £280 and the cost of the tickets was £8 per pupil. The school contributed part of the total cost. Each pupil paid £12. What fraction of the total cost was contributed by the school?

58. There were 27 pupils in a Year 8 history class.

    One pupil was absent when there was a mid-term test. The mean score for the group was 56.

    On returning to school the pupil who had been absent took the test and scored 86.

    What was the revised mean test score?

    Give your answer correct to one decimal place.

59. A school report includes the school's grades for each pupil's attainment in each subject.

    Grade A is awarded for an average test mark of 75% and above.

    The table below shows the results for an English test for a group of 24 pupils.

Pupil	Mark	Pupil	Mark
A	31	M	7
B	34	N	15
C	12	O	31
D	17	P	23
E	29	Q	26
F	19	R	28
G	24	S	29
H	30	T	33
I	32	U	29
J	28	V	34
K	25	W	30
L	33	X	28

    If the test was marked out of 36, how many pupils achieved a grade A?

60. An art teacher plans to take a group of 66 GCSE pupils together with a number of accompanying adults to an art gallery and museum.

Questions

The admission charges are as follows.

	Adults	Students
Art gallery	£8.50	£4.50
Museum	£5.50	£3.50
Combined ticket	£12.00	£6.00

One adult is admitted free when accompanying 30 students.

The group visits both the art gallery and the museum.

(a) How much is saved on the total student admission costs by buying combined tickets?

The school requires a ratio of at least 1 adult for every 20 students on educational visits.

(b) What is the cost of the combined tickets for the adults taking into account the free places they will get?

61. A teacher is planning a visit to an activity centre with a group of students. They will use the school minibus.

The round trip is approximately 200 miles. The fuel consumption for the minibus is 32 miles per gallon. The minibus uses diesel fuel which costs £1.34 per litre.

1 gallon = 4.546 litres

What is the estimated fuel cost for the visit? Give your answer to the nearest pound.

62. To inform a staff meeting a teacher prepared a table comparing pupils' results at level 5 and above in maths and science following end of Year 9 tests.

There were 120 boys and 112 girls in Year 9.

Number of pupils achieving at each level

Subject		Level 5	Level 6	Level 7
English	Boys	20	48	32
	Girls	10	48	40
Mathematics	Boys	20	56	32
	Girls	12	52	32
Science	Boys	20	56	36
	Girls	16	52	32

(a) In which subject was the percentage of boys achieving level 6 and above greater than the percentage of girls achieving level 6 and above?

(b) What proportion of pupils did not achieve a level 5 or above in English in the tests? Give your answer as a decimal to two decimal places.

4.5 Interpreting and using written data

Notes

Some terms, concepts and forms of representation which are used in statistics may be unfamiliar. The following notes are intended to give a brief summary of some of the unfamiliar aspects.

Some of the information received by schools, for example analyses of pupil performance, uses 'cumulative frequencies' or 'cumulative percentages'. One way to illustrate cumulative frequencies is through an example. The table shows the marks gained in a test by the 60 pupils in a year group.

22	13	33	31	51	24	37	83	39	28
31	64	23	35	9	34	42	26	68	38
63	34	44	77	37	15	38	54	34	22
47	25	48	38	53	52	35	45	32	31
37	43	37	49	24	17	48	29	57	33
30	36	42	36	43	38	39	48	39	59

We could complete a tally chart and a frequency table.

Mark, m	Tally	Frequency
9	1	1
10	0	0
11	0	0
12	0	0
13	1	1

and so on

But 60 results are a lot to analyse and we could group the results together in intervals. A sensible interval in this case would be a band of 10 marks. This is a bit like putting the results into 'bins'.

	13	22	33	
		24	31, 37	
		28	39	
$0 \le m < 10$	$10 \le m < 20$	$20 \le m < 30$	$30 \le m < 40$	$40 \le m < 50$	etc.

Note that $\le$ means 'less than or equal to' and $<$ means 'less than', so $30 \le m < 40$ means all the marks between 30 and 40 including 30 but excluding 40.

Here are the marks grouped into a frequency table.

Mark, m	Frequency	Cumulative frequency
$0 \leq m < 10$	1	1
$10 \leq m < 20$	3	4
$20 \leq m < 30$	9	13
$30 \leq m < 40$	25	38
$40 \leq m < 50$	11	49
$50 \leq m < 60$	6	55
$60 \leq m < 70$	3	58
$70 \leq m < 80$	1	59
$80 \leq m < 90$	1	60

Note how the cumulative frequency is calculated:

$\leftarrow 4 = 1 + 3$

$\leftarrow 13 = 1 + 3 + 9$, i.e. $4 + 9$

$\leftarrow 38 = 1 + 3 + 9 + 25$, i.e. $13 + 25$

The last column 'Cumulative frequency' gives the 'running total' – in this case the number of pupils with less than a certain mark. For example, there are 38 pupils who gained less than 40 marks.

The values for cumulative frequency can be plotted to give a cumulative frequency curve as shown below.

Note that the cumulative frequency values are plotted at the right-hand end of each interval, i.e. at 10, 20, 30 and so on.

You can use a cumulative frequency curve to estimate the median mark: the median for any particular assessment is the score or level which half the relevant pupils exceed and half do not achieve.

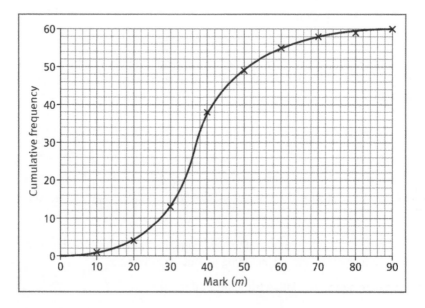

There are 60 pupils, so the median mark will be the 30th mark. (Find 30 on the vertical scale and go across the graph until you reach the curve and read off the value on the horizontal scale.) The median mark is about 37 – check that you agree.

It is also possible to find the quartiles. These are described in the Glossary on page 216.

The lower quartile will be at 25% of 60, that is the 15th value, giving a mark of about 31; the upper quartile is at 75% of 60, thus the 45th value, giving a mark of about 45.

The diagram below should further help to explain these terms. It also helps to introduce the idea of a 'box and whisker' plot.

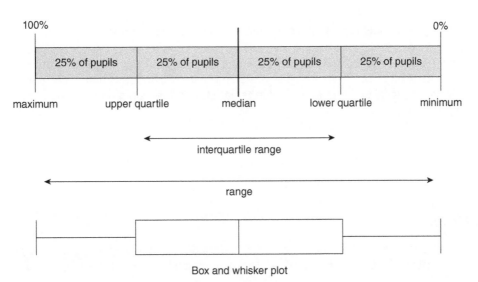

Box and whisker plot

The 'whiskers' indicate the maximum and minimum values, the ends of the 'box' the upper quartile and the lower quartile, and the median is shown by the line drawn across the box.

The 'middle 50%' of the values lie within the box and only the top 25% and the bottom 25% are outside the box. If the ends of the box are close together, then:

- the upper and lower quartiles are close, i.e. the interquartile range (that is the difference between them) is small;
- the slope of the cumulative frequency curve (or line) will be steep.

If the ends of the box are not close, then:

- the interquartile range is greater;
- the data is more 'spread out';
- the slope of the curve is less steep.

You need to interpret 'percentile' correctly: the 95th percentile does not mean the mark that 95% of the pupils scored but that 95% of the pupils gained that mark or lower – it is better perhaps to think that only 5% achieved a higher mark.

Example

Comparing a school's performance with national benchmarks, average NC levels

Percentile	95th	Upper quartile		60th	40th		Lower quartile		5th
English	4.26	4.1	**3.89**	3.89	3.78		3.56		3.36
Mathematics	4.25	3.92		3.85	3.63	**3.63**	3.59		3.24
Science	4.38	4.16		3.91	3.93		3.70	**3.54**	3.49

The figures in bold represent a particular school's average performance.

This table shows, for example, that 5% of pupils nationally gained higher than an average level of 4.26 in the English tests and that 40% of pupils nationally gained an average level of 3.63 or less in mathematics. In other words 60% gained a level higher than 3.63.

Questions

1. A secondary school has compared performance in the Key Stage 2 National Tests with performance at GCSE. The comparison is shown on the graph below.

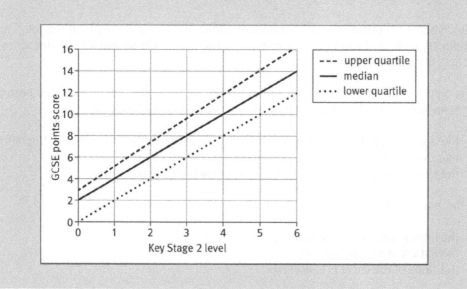

Questions

(a) What is the median GCSE points score of those pupils scoring a 2 at Key Stage 2?

(b) A pupil had a Key Stage 2 score of 5 and a GCSE points score of 11. Is it true to say that he was likely to be within the bottom 25% of all pupils?

(c) Is it true that 50% of the pupils who gained level 4 at Key Stage 2 gained GCSE points scores within the range 8 to 12?

2. For a department meeting, a head of mathematics produced a box and whisker graph comparing the performance in the end of year tests of four classes in year 7.

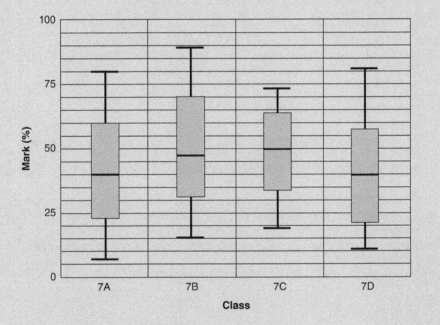

Indicate all the true statements:

A   The lowest mark was scored by a pupil in class 7D.

B   The median mark in class 7C was 10 marks higher than the median mark in class 7A.

C   In class 7B one quarter of the pupils achieved a mark of 70% or more.

3. A German language teacher compared the results of a German oral test and a German written test given to a group of 16 pupils.

Questions

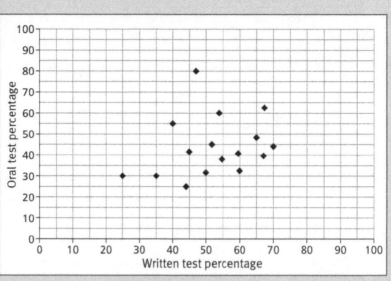

Indicate all the true statements.

A   The range of marks for the oral test is greater than for the written test.

B $\frac{1}{4}$ of pupils achieved a higher mark on the oral test than on the written test.

C   The two pupils with the lowest marks on the written test also gained the lowest marks on the oral test.

4. A teacher compared the result of an English test taken by all Year 8 pupils.

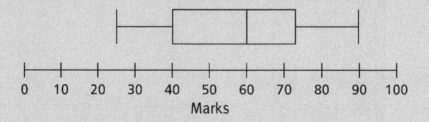

Indicate all the true statements.

A $\frac{1}{4}$ of all pupils scored more than 70 marks.

B $\frac{1}{2}$ of all pupils scored less than 60 marks.

C   The range of marks was 65.

5. In 2016 a survey was made of the nightly TV viewing habits of 10-year-old children in town A and town B. The findings are shown in the pie charts below:

Questions

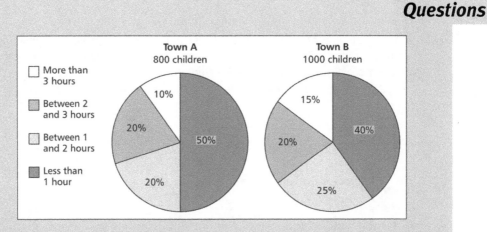

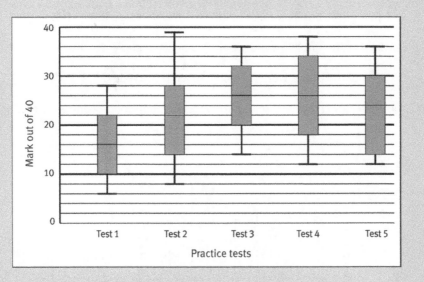

Use these pie charts to identify which of the following statements is true.

A   More children in town A watched TV for less than 1 hour than in town B.

B   More children in town B watched for between 2 and 3 hours than in town A.

C   100 children watched more than 3 hours in town A.

6. A teacher kept a box and whisker diagram to profile the progress of her class in practice tests. There are 16 pupils in the class.

(a) In which test did 12 students achieve 20 or more marks?

(b) Indicate all the true statements.

    A   The highest mark was achieved in test 2.

    B   The median mark increased with each test.

    C   The range of marks in test 3 and test 4 was the same.

Questions

7. At the beginning of Year 11 pupils at a school took an internal test which was used to predict GCSE grades in mathematics. From the results the predicted grades were plotted on a cumulative frequency graph.

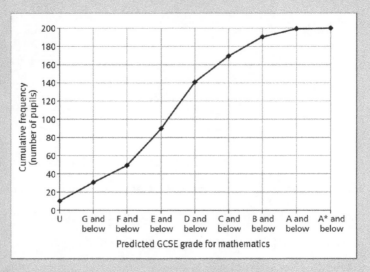

Indicate the true statement.

A   30% of the pupils were predicted to achieve grade C.

B   85% of the pupils were predicted to achieve grade C.

C   15% of the pupils were predicted to achieve grade C.

8. This bar chart shows the amount of pocket money children in Year 7 receive.

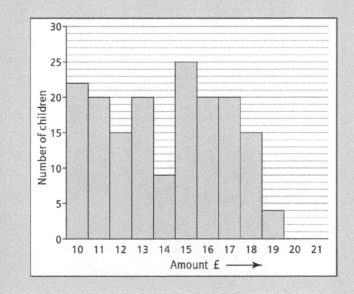

Questions

(a) How many children were surveyed?

(b) What is the modal amount of pocket money received?

9. A teacher recorded the marks given to five pupils in a series of mental arithmetic tests. Each test was based on 25 questions with 1 mark awarded for each correct answer.

Pupil	Test 1	Test 2	Test 3	Test 4
V	16	16	17	18
W	15	17	16	19
X	14	16	18	18
Y	16	17	18	18
Z	11	13	15	17

Indicate all the true statements.

A   The marks for all the pupils increased steadily

B   Pupil Z could be expected to gain a mark of 19 in the next test.

C   The mean, the median and the mode have the same value for test 4.

10. A Year 7 teacher was given information from feeder primary schools about pupils in the tutor group.

The two box plots below show the reading scores for two feeder schools A and B.

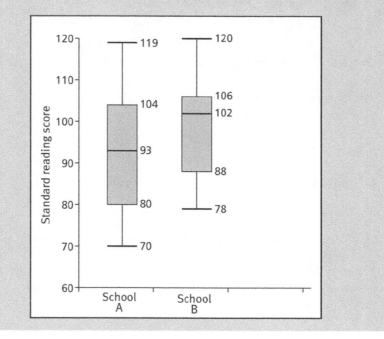

Questions

A standard reading score of 100 shows that a pupil's reading score was exactly on the national average for pupils of the same age. Standard scores of more than 100 show above average reading scores and below 100 show below average reading scores for pupils of the same age.

Indicate all the true statements.

A   The difference in the median scores for the two feeder schools was 9.

B   The interquartile range of the scores for school B was 18.

C   The range of scores was 9 less for school B than for school A.

11. Use the box plots and the information from question 10 to indicate the true statements.

A   50% of the pupils in school A had a reading score of 93 or more.

B   25% of pupils in school B scored 88 or less.

C   The interquartile range for the two schools was the same.

12. A research project compared the performance of Year 9 pupils taught mathematics, science and English in mixed classes or in single sex classes.

This table shows the results.

The median mark has been rounded to the nearest 10%.

| | Median mark achieved | | |
Subject	Boys only classes	Girls only classes	Mixed classes
English	50%	60%	60%
Mathematics	50%	60%	50%
Science	50%	50%	40%

Indicate all the true statements:

A   The single-sex groups produced better results in Science.

B   The mixed classes produced better results in English.

C   In mathematics, girls achieved higher scores than in mixed classes.

13. A mathematics teacher prepared a scatter graph to compare the results of pupils' performance in two tests. There were 24 pupils in the class.

Questions

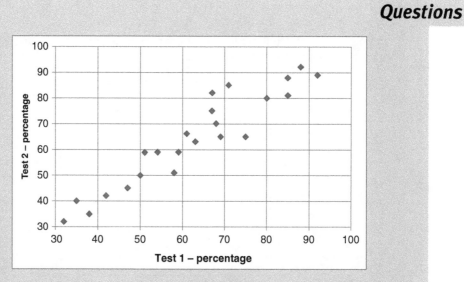

Indicate all the true statements:

A   6 pupils showed no improvement between the two tests.

B   A pupil who scored 71 in test 1 showed the greatest improvement in test 2.

C   9 pupils gained a lower percentage in test 2 than in test 1.

14. This box and whisker diagram shows the GCSE results in four subjects for a school in 2013.

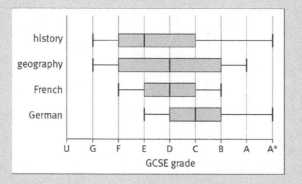

Indicate all the true statements.

A   50% of the pupils who took history gained grades F to C.

B   French had the lowest median grade.

C   50% of the pupils who took German gained grades C to A*.

Questions

15. The marks of ten students in the two papers of a German examination were plotted on this scatter graph:

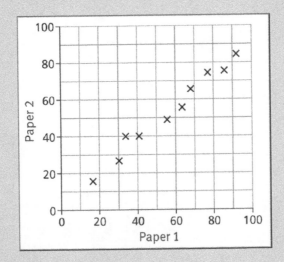

A student scored 53 marks on Paper 1 but missed Paper 2. What would you estimate her mark to be on Paper 2?

16. The straight line shows the mean levels scored in Year 9 assessments for a school plotted against the total GCSE points scores. The points A, B, C, D show the achievement of four pupils.

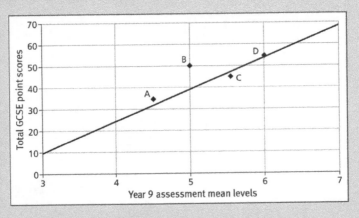

Indicate all the true statements.

A   Pupil D achieved as well as might have been predicted at GCSE.

B   Pupil C achieved a higher level in the Year 9 assessments than Pupil B but scored fewer points at GCSE than Pupil B.

C   At GCSE Pupil B achieved better than might have been predicted but Pupil A achieved less well than might have been predicted.

17. At a staff meeting teachers were shown a table showing the proportion of pupils achieving at least half marks in the end of Year 9 tests.

	Year			
Proportion of pupils achieving at least half marks in:	2013 (%)	2014 (%)	2015 (%)	2016 (%)
English	75.8	76.3	75.8	76.5
Mathematics	69.6	70.2	70.8	71.4
Science	59.0	61.2	62.8	64.0

Indicate all the true statements.

A   The greatest year on year improvement was for science between 2013 and 2014.

B   All subjects achieved a year-on-year improvement over the four-year period.

C   The smallest improvement over the four-year period was for English.

18. 20 pupils in a class took Test A at the beginning of a term and Test B at the end of the term.

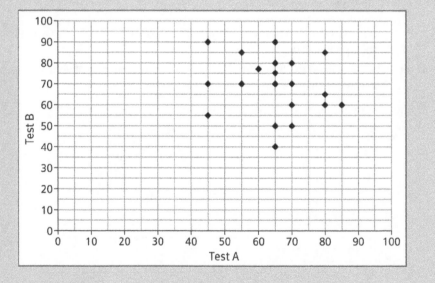

Indicate all the true statements.

A   The range of marks was wider for Test A than for Test B.

B   The lowest mark in Test A was lower than the lowest mark in Test B.

C   40% of the pupils scored the same mark or lower in Test B than in Test A.

D   More pupils scored over 60% in Test A than in Test B.

Questions

19. A teacher analysed the reading test standardised scores of a group of pupils.

Pupil	Gender	Age 8+ test standardised score	Age 10+ test standardised score
A	F	100	108
B	M	78	89
C	M	88	92
D	M	110	102
E	F	102	110
F	F	88	84
G	M	119	128
H	F	80	84

Indicate all the true statements.

A   All the girls improved their standardised scores between the Age 8+ and the Age 10+ tests.

B   The greatest improvement between the Age 8+ and the Age 10+ tests was achieved by a boy.

C $\frac{1}{4}$ of all the pupils had lower standardised scores in the Age 10+ tests than in the Age 8+ tests.

20. A teacher produced the following chart to show performance of year 11 pupils in GCSE mathematics in 2016

There were 200 pupils in the year group.

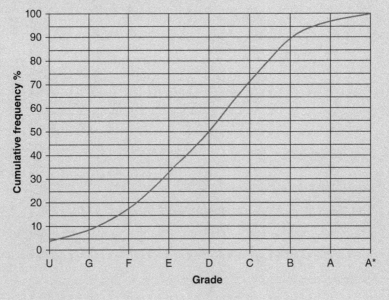

Questions

The number of pupils who achieved a grade B and above in mathematics was:

(a) 90

(b) 75

(c) 50

21. Schools in a federation analysed the percentages of pupils gaining 5 A*–C grades in their GCSE examinations over a six-year period. The results are shown in this table.

	Percentage of pupils gaining 5 A*–C grades					
School	2009	2010	2011	2012	2013	2014
A	47.9	48.6	54.7	54.6	55.8	58.4
B	64.5	64.8	65.0	65.2	65.4	65.6
C	66.1	65.3	64.3	63.7	63.5	63.0
D	49.7	54.7	57.0	63.6	63.7	63.8
E	58.3	59.1	58.5	59.3	58.7	59.5

Which schools improved each year over the six-year period?

22. A research project compared the performance of Year 9 pupils taught mathematics, science and English in mixed classes or in single-sex classes.

This table shows the results.

	Median level achieved		
Subject	Boys only classes	Girls only classes	Mixed classes
English	7	8	8
Mathematics	7	8	7
Science	7	7	6

Indicate all the true statements.

A   The single-sex groups produced better results in science.

B   The mixed classes produced better results in English.

C   In mathematics girls achieved higher scores than in mixed classes.

23. At a staff meeting teachers were shown a table showing the proportion of pupils achieving level 6 and above in the end of Year 9 tests.

Questions

Proportion of pupils achieving level 6 and above in:	Year			
	2011 (%)	2012 (%)	2013 (%)	2014 (%)
English	75.8	76.3	75.8	76.5
Mathematics	69.6	70.2	70.8	71.4
Science	59.0	61.2	62.8	64.0

Indicate all the true statements.

A   The greatest year-on-year improvement was for science between 2011 and 2012.

B   All subjects achieved a year-on-year improvement over the four-year period.

C   The smallest improvement over the four-year period was for English.

24. For a department meeting a head of mathematics produced a box and whisker graph comparing the performance in the end of year tests of four classes in Year 7.

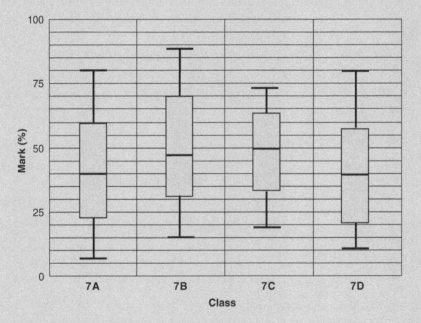

Indicate all the true statements.

A.   The range of marks for class 7A is the same as the range of marks for class 7B.

B.   50% of each class scored 40 marks or more.

C.   50% of class C scored 50 marks or less.

4.6 Answers and key points

4.2 Key knowledge

1. (a) $\dfrac{2}{3}$ (b) $\dfrac{3}{5}$ (c) $\dfrac{3}{4}$ (d) $\dfrac{3}{5}$

Key point
Remember to cancel down until there is no common factor for the numerator and denominator. Also, you ought to know that $\dfrac{75}{100}$ is $\dfrac{3}{4}$

2. (a) 0.15   (b) 0.36   (c) 0.65   (d) 0.02

Key point
Remember to change a percentage into a decimal divide by 100. The rule you may have been given at school, when dividing by 100, is "move the decimal point 2 places to the left".

3. (a) 70   (b) 10.35   (c) 162   (d) 22.5

Key point
Do the multiplication, ignoring any decimal points, then insert the decimal point counting from right to left the number of decimal places in the question. Thus $0.6 \times 342 \rightarrow 6 \times 342 = 2052$. There is 1 decimal figure so $0.6 \times 342 = 205.2$

4. (a) 96   (b) 90   (c) 9   (d) 48

Key point
Change each percentage into a decimal.

5. (a) 45   (b) 40   (c) 48   (d) 210

Key point
Either change fractions into decimals and then multiply or multiply by the numerator and then divide by the denominator

Answers

6. (a) 37.5%   (b) 80%   (c) 44%   (d) 80%

Key point
To change into a percentage multiply by 100% and this can be written as $\frac{100}{1}$.
Always try to simplify by looking for common factors

(a) $\frac{3}{8} \times \frac{100}{1} = 3 \times 12.5\% = 37.5\%$ (b) $\frac{4}{5} \times \frac{100}{1} = 4 \times 20\% = 80\%$

(c) $\frac{11}{25} \times \frac{100}{1} = 11 \times 4\% = 44\%$ (d) $\frac{28}{35} \times \frac{100}{1} = \frac{28}{7} \times 20\% = 4 \times 20\% = 80\%$

7. (a) $\frac{17}{20}$ (b) $\frac{3}{10}$ (c) $\frac{16}{25}$ (d) $\frac{3}{50}$

Key point
Cancel down – look for common factors, for example $85\% = \frac{85}{100}$ and dividing both
numbers by 5 gives $\frac{85}{100}$

4.3 Mental arithmetic

1. 55 minutes

Key point
Count on from 1 hour 20 minutes.

2. 28

Key point
70% of 40 = 0.7 x 40 or $\frac{7}{10} \times 40$

3. 17

Key point
Note: $100 \div 6 = 16.666$ therefore 17

Answers

4. 75%

Key point
The calculation is 3 x 28 = 84, then $(63 \div 84) \times 100$. Note: in a mental arithmetic test the fractions will cancel easily, as here to $\frac{3}{4}$.

5. 9

Key point
Note: $450 \div 52 = 8.65$, therefore 9

6. 48

Key point
Calculate as $30 \div 5 = 6$, then $6 \times 8 = 48$ or $8 \div 5 = 1.6$ so $30 \times 1.6 = 3 \times 16 = 48$

7. 12:40

Key point
Count on 1 hour 10 minutes + 2 hours.

8. 11

Key point
10 rows for 400 people, so one more row needed for the remaining 32

9. 84%

Key point
21 hours remaining $= \frac{21}{25} = 84\%$

10. £50

Key point
The quickest way to answer this is: double 94 giving 188, half of 94 is 47. So $94 \times £2.50 = £188 + £47 = £235$. Subtract from £285 gives £50.

Answers

11. 8%

Key point
Remember: to convert fractions with denominators of 25 to a percentage, multiply the numerator by 4: $\frac{22}{25} = 88\%$, therefore 8% difference.

12. £500

Key point
Simplify quickly by changing into £: 200 x 50 x 5p = £2 x 50 x 5

13. 60%

Key point
Fraction is $\frac{42}{70}$. Common factor is 7 giving $\frac{6}{10} = 60\%$

14. 720p or £7.20

Key point
Work out as 120 x 2 x 3 = 120 x 6

15. 0.075

Key point
Think of $7\frac{1}{2}\%$ as 7.5% then divide by 100.

16. 15

Key point
Work out as $\frac{3}{7}$ x 35

17. 265

Key point
(5 x 25) + (5 x 28)

Answers

18. 22 hours and 5 minutes

> **Key point**
> 5 x (4hr 25 mins) = (5 x 4hr) + (5 x 25 min) = 20hr + 125mins =20hr + 2hr 5 mins

19. 68%

> **Key point**
> 18 marks out of 25 plus 16 marks out of 25 gives 34 marks out of 50. Doubling gives 68 out of 100 which is 68%.

20. 36

> **Key point**
> First calculate 80% of 120 which is 0.8 x 120 = 96 (so 96 pupils achieved level 4 or level 5). Then subtract the pupils who achieved level 5, that is 60 pupils, leaving 36.

21. 1 hour 10 minutes

> **Key point**
> The calculation is 3hr – 1hr 50 mins

22. 0.625

> **Key point**
> The fraction is $\frac{54}{144}$. You now need to simplify this. You might recognise that 18 is a common factor, but if not then divide by 2 giving $\frac{27}{72}$ and then by 9 giving $\frac{3}{8}$. This then is the fraction who travel by bus. Therefore the fraction who don't travel by bus is $\frac{5}{8}$ and you should recognise this as 0.625. Alternatively you could first find the number who don't travel by bus, 144 – 54 = 90. Then express that as a fraction, $\frac{90}{144}$, divide by 16 or keep dividing by 2, and get $\frac{5}{8}$ which is 0.625.

23. $6.25m^2$

> **Key point**
> The calculation is 2.5 x 2.5. You should know that 25^2 is 625.

Answers

24. 12

Key point
Quicker to find 40% or $0.4 \times 30 = 12$

25. 9

Key point
Either work out the number staying on $= 0.7 \times 30 = 21$ and then subtract from 30 giving 9, or subtract first, those leaving $= 0.3$ and $0.3 \times 30 = 9$

26. 63

Key point
The calculation is $0.2 \times 315 = 63$.

27. 16

Key point
$31 \div 4 = 7\frac{3}{4}$ so 8 groups needed, $8 \times 2 = 16$

28. 56%

Key point
With 25 as the denominator you should know that you multiply the numerator by 4.

29. 14

Key point
Find $\frac{1}{5}$ and double to give $\frac{2}{5} \times 35 = 14$

30. 24%

Key point
Either – fraction gaining half marks or more $= \frac{19}{25}$ and $\frac{19}{25} \times \frac{100\%}{1} = 76\%$ so 24% gained less. Or 6 gained less so $\frac{6}{25} \times \frac{100\%}{1} = 24\%$

Answers

31. 0.125

Key point
Write it as 12.5 and divide by 100.

32. 405.6

Key point
Simple to multiply by 100 but be careful!

33. 60%

Key point
Either start with the fraction $\frac{2}{5}$ who don't speak English. This is equivalent to 40% so 60% speak English, or work with $\frac{3}{5}$ who do speak English and this is 60%.

34. 09:35 or 0935

Key point
Treat 40 minutes as 30 minutes + 10 minutes, i.e. 8:55 $\longrightarrow$ 9:25 $\longrightarrow$ 9:35

35. 110

Key point
20% + 25% = 45% so 55% play football

36. £100

Key point
Cost of 2 nights = €55 × 2 = €110. Divide by 1.1 gives £100

37. $\frac{2}{3}$

Key point
Either find the number who do stay in full-time education. This is $144 - 48 = 96$. Then express this as a fraction and simplify it: $\frac{96}{144} = \frac{8}{12} = \frac{2}{3}$. Or express those who do not stay in full-time education as a fraction and subtract. Thus $\frac{48}{144} = \frac{1}{3}$ so $\frac{2}{3}$ stay.

Answers

38. £19.20

> **Key point**
> The calculation is $2 \times 24 \times 0.4$

39. 2 days

> **Key point**
> 0.4×5 days = 2 days

40. 500

> **Key point**
> The calculation is $20 \times 25 = 500$

41. 3

> **Key point**
> $12\frac{1}{2}\%$ is $\frac{1}{8}$ – you should know this. $\frac{1}{8}$ of 24 = 3

42. 16:40 or 1640

> **Key point**
> 2×25 minutes = 50 minutes + 5 minutes = 55 minutes – i.e. 5 minutes less than 1 hour. So 1545 + 1 hour = 1645, subtract 5 minutes gives 1640

43. £257.60

> **Key point**
> Find 10% of £224 = £22.40. Find 5% by halving the 10% answer = £11.20. Add these to get £33.60. £224 + £33.60 = £257.60

44. £540

> **Key point**
> $365 - 5 = 360 \times £1.50 = 360 \times £1 + 360 \times £0.5 = £360 + £180$

45. 0.9kg

> **Key point**
> The area = $3 \times 3 = 9$ square metres x 100g = 900g which is 0.9kg.
>
> Remember that there are 1000g in a kg.

4.4 Solving written arithmetic problems

1. Mean = 29.7; mode = 24; range = 17

> **Key point**
> $$\text{Mean} = \frac{19 \times 2 + 24 \times 8 + 27 \times 1 + 29 \times 5 + 33 \times 2 + 34 \times 5 + 36 \times 7}{30} = \frac{890}{30} = 29.7$$
> Mode = most frequent mark, not the number of times it occurs.

2. £87.72

> **Key point**
> $€100 = £\dfrac{100}{1.14} = £87.719$. Remember that money has only 2 decimal places so round up to £87.72

3. 25

> **Key point**
> 30 pupils scored either 100 or 101. Ratio is 5:1. Divide 30 by (5 + 1) = 5 so 1 part = 5 so 25 pupils scored 100 (and 5 scored 101)

4. School A

> **Key point**
> Score of 100 or 101. School A = $\dfrac{22}{33} = 66.7\%$; School B = $\dfrac{21}{32} = 65.6\%$.
> School C = $\dfrac{23}{35} = 65.7\%$

5. 10 below

> **Key point**
> Find 18% of 250 = 0.18 × 250 = 45, so 10 below

6. C is true

> **Key point**
> You need to calculate the total number of pupils for each year – 2016 has 42, 2015 has 35, 2014 has 48, 2013 has 48.
> A% gaining A or B in 2013 is $\dfrac{37}{48} = 77\%$. In 2016 it is $\dfrac{34}{42} = 52\%$, so not true.
> B In 2015, % failing to get A = $\dfrac{21}{35} = 60\%$. In 2014 it is $\dfrac{25}{48} = 52\%$, so not true.
> C Gaining A in 2016 = $\dfrac{19}{42} = 45\%$. In 2015 it is $\dfrac{14}{35} = 40\%$, so true.

Answers

7. 3

Key point
25% of 6 hours is 1 hour 30 minutes so 2 sessions (80 minutes) is too short.

8. A

Key point
The calculation is $(\frac{58}{75} \times 0.6) + (\frac{65}{125} \times 0.4) = 0.464 + 0.208 = 0.672$, i.e. 67.2%

9. Test 3

Key point
Convert to percentages.

10. 7PH and 7TM

Key point
You need to calculate $\frac{2}{3}$ of the numbers in each class. Only 7PH and 7TM have more pupils attending than $\frac{2}{3}$ of the class totals.

11. A and B are true

Key point
By inspection you can save time. A mean score of 16 cannot come from pupils B and C – the highest score for B is 15 and for C is 14.

12. (a) 1%   (b) 2014

Key point
(a) in 2015 $\frac{84}{110} = 76.4\%$ ie 76%. Target was 75%

(b) work out and compare the percentages for 2012–2015

For 2015 it is 1%; for 2014 it is $\frac{82}{104} = 78.8\%$ – i.e. 79%, giving 3%; for 2013 it is $\frac{74}{98} = 75.5\%$ – i.e. 76%, giving 1%; for 2012, it is $\frac{70}{94} = 74.5\%$ – i.e. 75%, giving 1%

13. A and B are true

Key point
Remember that e.g. $-3 < d \leq -6$ means that the difference, d, cannot be -3 but could lie between -3.1 and -6.

Answers

(a) Boys is $1 + 3 + 3 + 2 = 9$. Girls is $1 + 1 + 2$.

(b) Girls is $1 + 3 + 3 + 2 = 9$, so proportion $= \dfrac{9}{15} = 0.6$.

(c) We do not know exactly how many are 12 months or more above their actual age.

14. School Q

Key point
Change each figure into decimals:

$\dfrac{2}{9} = 0.222$ 57 out of 300 = 0.19   18% = 0.18

15. 11

Key point
Look at the second table. To score a scaled score of less than 100, the marks have to be less than 59.

16. 4.5

Key point
Use a ruler to help – find 6 on the horizontal axis and read off the corresponding value on the vertical axis.

17. 28%

Key point
Because the times both involve half hours, it is simply working out $\dfrac{6.5}{23.5}$ x 100 = 27.66% = 28% to the nearest per cent.

18. 50%

Key point
Subtract, remembering 12 months in a year. Pupils A, C, E, G, H fit the criterion.

19. $\dfrac{35}{60} = \dfrac{7}{12}$

Key point
Count pupil numbers carefully – jot down totals.

Answers

20. 15

> **Key point**
>
> $1500 \div 100 = 15$

21. a

> **Key point**
>
> Number of 'pupil laps' = $(65 \times 8 + 94 \times 10) = 1460$
>
> Total distance = $1460 \times 700 = 1022\,000$ metres = $1\,022$km

22. 10

> **Key point**
>
> Use a sketch – 3 small sheets per width of large sheet.

23. (a) 35   (b) 39

> **Key point**
>
> (a)   remember to order the percentage marks
>
> (b)   total = $36 + 47 + 34 + 33 + 45 = 195$ so mean is $195 \div 5 = 39$

24. a

> **Key point**
>
> For a: 2013 has 3/28 = 10.7%; 2014 has 11/34 = 32.4%; 2015 has 11/40 = 27.5%; 2016 has 11/36 = 30.6%. Note 2014, 2015 and 2016 all have 11 pupils gaining A or A* so the biggest % is when the denominator of each fraction is smallest – if you spot this you can save some time.
>
> For b: the fractions are: 11/28; 13/34; 16/40; 10/36 and 16/40 is a higher % than the others.
>
> For c: finding $\frac{1}{4}$ of the pupil numbers gives in 2013 →7, 2 is less than 7, in 2014→ 8.5, but 9 is more than 8.5 so statement c is not true.

25. (a) 192km   (b) 31 miles (actually 31.25)

> **Key point**
>
> The calculations are: (a) $120 \times \frac{8}{5}$ (b) $50 \times \frac{5}{8}$

Answers

26. 0.1mm

> **Key point**
> Take care with the units – work in millimetres, i.e. $50 \div 500$.

27. 33%

> **Key point**
> The fraction is $\dfrac{20}{60}$ so as a percentage this is 33.3333%, i.e. 33% to the nearest whole number.

28. 128cm

> **Key point**
> You can fit 8 lots of 15cm across the 120cm width.

29. 5:30 a.m.

> **Key point**
> Remember time = distance ÷ speed. The travel time = $120 \div 40 = 3$ hours. Add 0.5 hour, therefore total time = 3.5 hours.

30. 16km

> **Key point**
> Total map distance = 32.3cm = 32.3 x 50 000cm on the ground = 16.15km

31. 363.6 seconds = 6 minutes 3.6 seconds

> **Key point**
> Add up the time in seconds and decimals of seconds giving 363.6 seconds then convert.

32. £65.88; £83.88

> **Key point**
> Remember to work in £ on the mileage rate.

Answers

33. 28 pupils

> **Key point**
> From 9:00 to 10:30 is 90 minutes ⟶ she can see 4 pupils.
> From 10:45 to 12:00 is 75 minutes ⟶ she can see 3 pupils.
> Total for the day = 7 pupils, total over 4 days = 28 pupils.
> If the calculations were done using the total figures:
> > her working week = 4 x 3 hours less 4 x 15 minutes = 11 hours
> > 11 hours = 660 minutes ÷ 20, giving 33 pupils
> This would be incorrect because it ignores the 'structure' of the school morning.

34. 1.514m

> **Key point**
> The total height for the 20 girls = 20 x 1.51 = 30.2m
> The new total height = 30.2 + 1.6 = 31.8 m but this is for 21 girls
> The new mean height = 31.8 ÷ 21= 1.514m

35. (a) Test 1   (b) 0.3

> **Key point**
> (a) The range for test 1 is –10 to 10 which is 20.
> > The range for test 2 is –9 to 10 which is 19.
> > So test 1.
> (b) 5 pupils made no progress so as a fraction this is $\frac{5}{16}$ which equals 0.3125. This rounds to 0.3.

36. 8 layers

> **Key point**
> The calculation, working in centimetres, is 124 ÷ 15 = 8.266, so round down.

37. 18

> **Key point**
> There are two ways of solving this: The first way would be to (a) find the number studying maths. This is 20% of 150 = 30. (b) find the number studying chemistry – 8% of 150 = 12, and then find the difference: 30 – 12 = 18.

Answers

The second way would be to find the difference in the percentages: $20\% - 8\% = 12\%$. Then find 12% of 150 = 18.

38. 11:20

Key point
400km = 250 miles

39. A

Key point
A raw score of 52 gives from the graph a UMS value of 76. From the table this results in a grade A.

40. 25

Key point
Sample size = 10 + 150 ÷ 10 = 25

41. A and B are true

Key point
Remember to go down columns for maths and French, and along rows for English.

A   Number gaining A* – C in French is 20 + 40 = 60 out of a total of 80.

$\% = \dfrac{60}{80} = 75\%$.

B   In the maths table, 38 gained A*–A in English and 57 gained B–C, so 38 + 57 = 95 gained C or above in English. This is more than half of 120.

C   In French, 16 + 3 + 1 = 20 did not achieve a grade C or above. This is $\dfrac{1}{4}$ of 80 so not true.

42. B, E, G, H

Key point
Find 5% of 120 = 6 so look for marks in test 2 that are 6 marks higher than in test 1.

43. 72

Key point
Remember to work out brackets first and to round up.

Answers

44. 55

45. b and c are true

46. 53

47. 30

48. 98

49. 7.5km/h

Answers

50. 23.67

Key point
You must work out $20 \div 15$ first, not 25×20 then divide by 15.
Therefore reading level $= 5 + (20 - 1.33) = 5 + 18.67 = 23.67$

51. 5.51

Key point
The total points are given by $(4 \times 5) + (4 \times 6) + (1 \times 7) + (1 \times 8) = 59$
The calculation is then $(\frac{59}{10} \times 3.9) - 17.5 = 5.51$

52. 87

Key point
The calculation is $80 = A \times 0.6 + 70 \times 0.4$
$$80 = A \times 0.6 + 28$$
Therefore $\quad A \times 0.6 = 52$
$$A = 52 \div 0.6 = 86.67, \text{ i.e. } 87$$

53. A is true

Key point
Remember that the table lists %.
A   35% gained A*–A. 35% of 80 = 28, so true.
B   8% of 25 = 2; 5% of 60 = 3, so not true
C   80 gained A*–C in English. 42 gained A*–A , so not true.

54. 18

Key point
$\frac{3}{4} - \frac{1}{2} = \frac{1}{4}$ so $\frac{1}{4}$ receive an award.

55. 9.6

Key point
Work out brackets first.

Answers

56. B and C are true

> **Key point**
>
> A   School A had no change in 2014, 2015.
>
> B   Range of values for 2013–16: A is 5 percentage points, B is 24, C is 13 and D is 12.
>
> C   School B is 81%; school D is 69%.

57. $\dfrac{1}{4}$

> **Key point**
>
> Cost = £280 + 35 × £8 = £560. Pupils pay 35 × £12 = £420. School pays £560 − £420 = £140. Fraction is $\dfrac{140}{560} = \dfrac{1}{4}$.

58. 57.1

> **Key point**
>
> Total for 26 pupils = 26 × 56 = 1456. New total = 1456 + 86 = 1542
>
> New mean = 1542 ÷ 27

59. 15

> **Key point**
>
> 75% of 36 = 27, so count pupils with a mark of 27 or more.

60. (a) £132   (b) £24

> **Key point**
>
> (a) The cost of separate tickets for 1 student is £4.50 + £3.50 = £8.00. So for 66 students the cost = 66 x £8.00 = £528. The cost of 66 combined tickets is 66 × £6 = £396. The saving is £528 – £396 = £132.
>
> (b) 66 students will require 4 adults (note: 3 adults will only 'cover' 60 students). 2 adults will be free – since 66 is greater than 60. So only 2 adults will have to pay. Cost = 2 × £12.00 = £24.00.

Answers

61. £38

Key point

The calculation can be broken down into stages:

- the number of gallons used $= \dfrac{200}{32} = 6.25$;
- the number of litres $= 6.25 \times 4.546 = 28.4125$;
- the cost $= 28.4125 \times £1.34 = £38.07$ which rounds to £38.

If you do these sorts of calculations try to avoid rounding any intermediate answers and round when you get the final answer.

62. (a) Science   (b) 0.15

Key point

(a) Maths:

  Number of boys @ levels 6 and 7 $= 56 + 32 = 88$

  Number of girls @ levels 6 and 7 $= 52 + 32 = 84$

  Total number of boys $= 120$; total number of girls $= 112$

  Therefore % boys $= \dfrac{88}{120} \times 100 = 73\%$

  % girls $= \dfrac{84}{112} \times 100 = 75\%$

  Science:

  Number of boys @ levels 6 and 7 $= 56 + 36 = 92$

  Number of girls @ levels 6 and 7 $= 52 + 32 = 84$

  Total number of boys $= 120$; total number of girls $= 112$

  Therefore % boys $= \dfrac{92}{120} \times 100 = 77\%$

  % girls $= \dfrac{84}{112} \times 100 = 75\%$

Thus in science the percentage of boys achieving level 6 and above was greater than the percentage of girls.

(b) Total number of boys achieving levels 5, 6 and 7 $= 20 + 48 + 32 = 100$

  Therefore $120 - 100 = 20$ did not.

  Total number of girls achieving levels 5, 6, and 7 $= 10 + 48 + 40 = 98$

  Therefore $112 - 98 = 14$ did not.

  Total who did not achieve levels 5, 6 and 7 $= 34$

  Total pupils $= 120 + 112 = 232$

  $\dfrac{34}{232} = 0.14655$ so 0.15

Answers

Chapter 4.5 Interpreting and using written data

1. (a) 6   (b) No   (c) Yes

> **Key point**
> (a) Find 2 on the Key Stage 2 axis and move up the graph until you reach the median line. Read off the value on the GCSE axis.
>
> (b) Find 11 on the GCSE axis and 5 on the Key Stage 2 axis. The lines through these values intersect in the space between the lower quartile line and the median line so it is not true – remember that 25% of the pupils are below the lower quartile.
>
> (c) Find 4 on the Key Stage 2 axis, 50% lie between 8 (the lower quartile) and 12 (the upper quartile).

2. B and C are true

> **Key point**
> A   Not true – the lowest mark is for class 7A at about 6 or 7 marks.
> B   True – the median for 7C is 50 and for 7A is 40.
> C   True – the upper quartile for 7B is at 70, so a quarter of the pupils scored 70 or more.

3. A and B are true.

> **Key point**
> A.   Oral range = 80 – 25 = 55; written range = 70 – 25 = 45.
> B.   Imagine a line drawn from (0, 0) to (100, 100). This is the line where scores on both tests were the same. There are 4 points above this line, $\frac{4}{16} = \frac{1}{4}$
> C.   Lowest written marks are 25 and 35, both pupils scoring 30 in the oral, but another pupil scored 25 in the oral.

4. B and C are true.

> **Key point**
> A.   This is false. The upper quartile is at 73, so 1/4 of all the pupils scored more than 73 marks, not 70.
> B.   Median is at 60 so true.
> C.   Range = 90 – 25 = 65 so true.

Answers

5. B is true.

It is important to realise that, although the pie charts appear to be the same size, they represent different 'quantities' – 800 children and 1000 children.

Statement A is not true. 50% of 800 = 40% of 1000

$\qquad$ (0.5 x 800 = 400 and 0.4 x 1000 = 400)

Statement B is true. 20% of 1000 is more than 20% of 800

$\qquad$ (0.2 X 1000 = 200, 0.2 X 800 = 160)

Statement C is not true. 10% of 800 = 80

6. (a) Test 3 $\qquad$ (b) Only A is true.

Key point
Remember that each 'part' of a box and whisker plot represents 25%.

7. Only C is true.

Key point
140 pupils get D and below, 170 get C and below so 30 get grade C.

8. (a) 170 $\qquad$ (b) £15

Key point
(a) Add up the values given by the tops of each bar:

$\qquad$ 22 + 20 + 15 + 20 + 9 + 25 + 20 + 20 + 15 + 4

(b) The modal amount is that received by the most children, i.e. £15 received by 25 children.

9. B and C are true.

Key point
A is not true. Pupils V, X and Y have 2 years with the same mark.

B is true – while it is unlikely the indications are that pupil Z's marks go up by 2 each test.

C is true – the mean is 18 – add the marks (=90) divide by 5. The median is 18 – the middle value when the marks are put in order – and the mode is 18.

Answers

10. A and B are true.

> **Key point**
> A. Medians are 102 and 93.
> B. Interquartile range for B = 106 − 88
> C. School A range = 119 − 70, school B range = 120 − 78

11. A and B are true.

> **Key point**
> A. 50% lie above the median line.
> B. 25% lie below the lower quartile.
> C. IQ range for A = 24 and for B = 18.

12. A and B are true

> **Key point**
> A   Is true – 50% for single-sex classes and 40% for mixed.
> B   Not true – mixed and girls only classes both at 60%.
> C   True – 60% for girls with 50% for boys only and mixed.

13. A and B are true

> **Key point**
> A   Is true – draw in the line of equal scores – i.e. join (30, 30) to (100, 100). There are 6 pupils on this line.
> B   True – pupil gained 85.
> C   Not true – 7 pupils below the line.

14. A and C are true.

> **Key point**
> A. History 'box' extends from F to C.
> B. History has a lower median grade.
> C. German median is at grade C so 50% gained C to A*.

Answers

15. About 45–49 marks

Key point
You need to draw in the line of best fit through the points.

16. A and B are true.

Key point
A.   D lies on the line.
B.   C is to the right of but below B.
C.   A is above the line so A also achieved better than might have been predicted.

17. A and C are true

Key point
A   True – in 2013–14, 61.2% – 59.0% = 2.2%.
B   Not true. English decreased in 2015.
C   English is 76.5% –75.8% = 0.7%; Maths is 71.4% –69.6% = 1.8%; Science is 64% –59% = 5%.

18. C and D are true.

Key point
A.   Range for A = 85 – 45 = 40, range for B = 90 – 40 = 50
B.   Lowest value for A = 45 and for B = 40
C.   Imagine a line drawn from (0, 0) to (100, 100), 8 pupils on or below the line and $\frac{8}{20}$ = 40%
D.   14 scored over 60% in Test A and 13 scored over 60% in Test B

19. B and C are true.

Key point
A.   Pupil F score decreased.
B.   Pupil B score increased by 11.
C.   Two pupils (D, F) had lower scores.

Answers

20. (c)

> **Key point**
> 75% gained grade C or below, so 25% gained a grade B, A or A*. 25% of 200 = 50.

21. Schools B and D

> **Key point**
> B and D are the only two schools with values increasing each year.

22. A and C are true.

> **Key point**
> A.   is true – level 7 in science for single-sex classes and 6 for the mixed classes.
> B.   is not true – the levels achieved for the girls only classes were the same as the mixed classes.
> C.   is true – the girls only classes achieved level 8 compared with level 7 for the mixed and the boys only classes.

23. A and C are true.

> **Key point**
> A.   is true – the actual increase is $61.2 - 59.0 = 2.2$
> B.   is not true – the English performance decreased in 2013
> C.   is true – for English the calculation is $76.5 - 75.8 = 0.7$
> For mathematics it is $71.4 - 69.6 = 1.8$
> For science it is $64.0 - 59.0 = 5.0$

24. A and C are true.

> **Key point**
> A.   is true – the range for class 7A is $80 - 6 = 74$. That for 7B is $89 - 15 = 74$.
> B.   is not true – the median for 7A and 7D are at 40, the medians for 7B and 7C are higher.
> C.   true – the median for 7C is at 50.

5 | Teacher training, applications and interviews

This chapter about teacher training, applications and interviews is divided into the following sections:

5.1 Is teacher training really for me?
5.2 What makes a good ITT application?
5.3 What makes a good ITT interview candidate?

For ease of reference, the chapter poses the sort of questions you may well be asking right now, followed by the typical responses that ITT providers might give.

5.1 Is teacher training really for me?

Think carefully about applying for ITT. Ask yourself the questions now: 'Is this really for me?' Consider what it is going to cost you in fees for the course. 'Will I be eligible for a bursary?' How will you manage to cope with the studying? This is obviously going to be a pretty big commitment on your part. Are you ready for it? Be honest with yourself – you've got to be certain that this is the right course for you.

We all have memories of teachers at school. Some teachers may even have inspired you in your choice of future profession. Others may have been terrible, scary or indifferent. What sort of teacher do you want to be? Do you want to be remembered by your pupils as successful, passionate, inspirational and fun?

Teaching is not an easy choice, but it can be extremely rewarding. Remember that being a good teacher doesn't happen overnight – you will need to be patient as you will have to work hard at it. Try to identify and improve your weaknesses, and continue to reinforce your strengths.

How much do my A level subjects count?

Your A-level subjects may give an indication of some of your strengths. However, not everyone comes via the A-level road. Some people enter BEds (or other degrees, than PGCEs) from college Access courses.

However, the current official minimum admission requirements for ITT are not A levels or GCSEs. They are either a level 3 qualification for BEds or a first degree for PGCE. Your A level subjects do not matter – it is the subject of your degree which is important. You do, however, need GCSEs (or equivalencies) in English and maths, and, if training for primary education, science.

How much does my degree subject count?

This varies across institutions. Many will look for a match between degree and the curriculum, so applicants should be ready to explain the relevance of their degree study to becoming a teacher. If you have a psychology degree, for example, you should emphasise that the skills you have developed are a good basis for teaching curriculum subjects such as maths and science. Provide clear examples.

Do I need to have experience in a school before applying?

The simple answer is 'yes'. And generally, the more experience the better. How can you really know that you want to become a teacher if you haven't been into a school? Gaining experience in a school is becoming essential as the government increases the role of schools in training. But it's not just about clocking up *experience:* it's about what you make of that time and what you take from it. There are several good reasons:

- **You are about to invest a year of your life and a lot of money in your ITT course. So you want to be *certain* that teaching is really what you want to do. You need to see close up what classroom life is like and what teachers actually have to do during, and out of, class time.**
- **You have to become *familiar* with the curriculum and the way in which schools work. School experience will give you an up-to-date basis of experience to build on by the time you start your course. Make sure you can discuss what you have done, observed and learned from your experiences.**
- **You need to know that you are able to function in a classroom. You will have to be *comfortable* taking on the mantle of 'teacher'. Some people, however strong their commitment to teaching, find it terribly difficult to step into that role. Early experience may help you to consider whether you are actually cut out for teaching. You need to be confident that you have made the right choice of career.**

Many teacher education programmes will expect at least ten days as an observer/helper prior to starting your course. Be prepared to answer questions about your time in school:

- **How do teachers manage their classrooms?**
- **How do teachers interest and engage pupils in learning?**

Think of other possible questions to do with your experiences in school and prepare suitable answers. You might want to practise answers aloud to ensure that you are clear, fluent and sound natural.

Do I have to be super confident and outgoing?

No. All types of personalities can be successful teachers. However, a school's personnel will be reassured if you appear reasonably confident and assertive. You do not need to be the most outgoing person in the world, but it will certainly help if you feel confident in your own abilities as a beginning trainee teacher. If you can develop the ability to engage learners – making learning fun – and are able to connect with the pupils in your class, they are much more likely to trust and respect you. Listening carefully to questions and responding to them sincerely and honestly are more impressive than super-abundant confidence. The ability to inspire pupils is a key requirement, but remember that you will develop plenty of skills as you yourself learn.

Should I be thick-skinned and able to take criticism?

If you are extremely thick-skinned, you probably won't listen to all the little things that you should be heeding. This means that you won't learn as much as you should – and you will certainly annoy people around you. However, if you are so sensitive that you see criticism almost everywhere, and if you mistakenly begin to translate that into 'people not liking you', then you will sink into self-doubt and anxiety. In such a tough environment it therefore stands to reason that you will need to find a happy middle ground.

Sift out what actually matters in what others say – acting on anything immediately if you need to – and then bounce back. That's resilience. The number one quality prized by those who supervise trainee teachers is for them to take on board what is said to them, and then to act on it *immediately*. Work hard, think positive and always be on time – in school placements these qualities can go a long way to avoiding unnecessary criticism.

Trainee teachers will have to be able to reflect critically on their own practice. They should also be willing to accept constructive criticism from others. Criticism from tutors and school-based mentors will be offered constructively with the sole intention of helping you to be the best teacher you can possibly be.

What qualities do I really need to succeed on an initial teacher training course?

Here are 12 important qualities in a trainee teacher or NQT:

- *Desire:* you will need to really want to teach children or young people.
- *Commitment:* you must be willing to work extremely hard – the training period is very intensive and demanding (but, for your own sanity, try to remember to maintain a healthy work-to-life balance!).
- *Resilience:* take the rough with the smooth, and bounce back.
- *Enthusiasm:* be an energetic learner yourself and pass on your own enthusiasm to your pupils.
- *Humility:* try to relate to your pupils and learn from them, rather than thinking that you're the one with all the knowledge.
- *Self-motivation:* constantly reflect on the quality and effectiveness of what you offer your pupils – see yourself as a perpetual learner and learn from all that you do.
- *Organisation:* manage your time well and keep well organised – you may need to juggle several balls at the same time during a teaching degree.
- *Awareness:* be aware of the reasons why you are required to do what you have to do.
- *Teamwork:* learn to work with others – be flexible in outlook and willing to change your ideas based on evidence.
- *Responsibility:* don't be afraid of taking risks and seeking responsibility – you won't learn by holding back or hiding behind others.
- *Initiative:* be an active, resourceful learner – it's not all handed to you on a plate.
- *Sense of humour:* stay cheerful and good humoured – make an effort to engage with your peers and tutors.

Time to reflect

The ideal trainee teacher and NQT is someone who is enthusiastic, knowledgeable, reflective – and is able to communicate effectively. You'll also need to be creative in your thinking. Have the confidence to believe in yourself and the flexibility to adapt your thoughts, ideas and teaching.

Be passionate about what you believe in and about your subject. This will always shine through. It's probably a good idea to look through the Teachers' Standards in order to gain an insight into what is expected as a trainee and as a teacher. High levels of academic competence are also required. Good teachers love working with children and young people in their care. Think about the positive effect you can have on your pupils' future lives – you can make a huge difference in your new role.

5.2 What makes a good ITT application?

When you are applying for a course it makes obvious sense that you need to present yourself in the best possible light. Distinguish yourself from other applicants by coming across as an outstanding candidate in your written application. Don't spoil your own chances of success with poor content or untidy presentation.

Spelling, punctuation and grammar don't matter that much, do they?

Yes they do. They are essential. Why? Because teachers are the models for pupils. If you are going to teach children how to spell and how to use punctuation and grammar correctly, it stands to reason that you will be proficient in these areas yourself.

Some ITT providers automatically discard applications that show that prospective students cannot be bothered to proof-read them. If someone cannot put in the effort at this stage, they certainly won't put in the necessary effort as a trainee or teacher. It is therefore important for you to make the right first impression, especially in such a competitive market. Work through your application carefully, using a dictionary to avoid spelling mistakes. Ask a friend or relative with strong literacy skills to check it for you.

If you are dyslexic you may make a very good teacher. Many dyslexic teachers manage to equip themselves with a range of effective strategies to make sure that they provide a good model for children in their care. Indeed, they are often at an advantage because they understand from first-hand experience many of the difficulties that pupils may have with literacy.

How much does the presentation of my application matter?

Presentation is every bit as important as spelling, punctuation and grammar. Your application must be well written, concise and it needs to address the important issues. Nowadays most applications are online, so it is important that font size and style is readable and appropriate. Dispense with smiley faces and emoticons!

What sort of thing should I include in my personal statement?

The content of the personal statement is very important. Keep it relevant and concise. Make sure that it:

- **shows your commitment to education;**
- **demonstrates your lively interest in how you as a teacher can help pupils to learn and develop;**

- **summarises some of your various talents and skills, showing clearly how these are relevant to teaching; and**
- **provides a flavour of you as a person.**

Ask yourself, why should anyone invite you to interview on the basis of this letter? Structure your application so that it doesn't become a long list of 'I did this, then I did that'. It is far better to have focused paragraphs which include select examples.

And remember not to fall into the trap of over-emphasising your wish to 'work with children', which in itself is not sufficient when applying for a *teaching* course. It's important to show an interest in children, but just make sure that you don't overdo it.

Do you want to know all about my bachelor's degree and what I have studied?

No, it's not really necessary to go through details of your bachelor's degree in your letter of application. You can include the important information on the form. In your personal statement, simply identify how you think your degree study has prepared you to enter the teaching profession. How has the experience developed you as a person, socially and intellectually? How does this relate to the skills and qualities that you believe are important in a teacher?

Do you need to know all about my previous studies?

Your previous studies will be listed in the appropriate sections of the application form, so there will be little value in restating this in your personal statement – unless it relates directly to teaching or working with children.

What about all the extra-curricular activities I have done?

Importantly, what do your extra-curricular activities say about you? Include these only if you can answer questions about how these have matured your outlook or will enhance your teaching ability. If you have been a sports coach, a summer school tutor, or been involved in musical activities, for example, these may have direct relevance to your curriculum knowledge, your teaching skills and your management of young people. This demonstrates that you can manage time successfully, prioritise and contribute to wider teams – all key skills for teachers. A history of working with children will strengthen your application and can show your suitability for the course. If, however, you state that your main interests are shopping or meeting up with friends, how will you be able to expand upon this convincingly at interview?

Are you interested in any travelling I may have done?

Yes, but think about what your travelling says about you as a person. Voluntary work overseas will count for more than a two-week package holiday in Ibiza. As always, pull out the most relevant features and explain exactly how they support your application. Keep it brief unless this was relevant work with children, such as Camp America or teaching EFL abroad.

Are you interested in any part-time jobs I have had?

Yes, if they have involved working with children or are of direct relevance to teaching. If not, you may still have transferable skills and qualities that will be beneficial as a student and class teacher. Emphasise skills you have developed dealing with the public, working as a member of a team, or taking responsibility for completing a task to high standards. You can mention good timekeeping and give examples of your ability to demonstrate a professional manner in the workplace.

Are you interested in my work history?

Interviewers will want to find out about your past career, if you are coming to ITT after working full time. Also, why are you ready to take a different pathway now? Do not leave big gaps in your cv – although interviewers may not necessarily probe areas like this, they may still be wary. If you are making a major career change, you should explain your motivation, and identify transferable skills or knowledge from your previous work. It is extremely important to have classroom experience to underpin a career change – you need to show that you are clear what the change involves, as teaching is never an easy option. For some applicants, it may be difficult to gain that classroom experience while working. Using annual leave to gain that experience can be a worthwhile sacrifice (and demonstrates a true commitment to teaching as your future career).

Do you want to know all about my political views and/or my views on the current controversies in education?

No, but an awareness of topical issues within education is important. Are you aware of government initiatives, policy and practice with regard to education? In 2015, the government published the *Prevent Duty Guidance*. This outlines duties of specified authorities to have due regard to the need to prevent people from being drawn into terrorism. All teachers in England need to understand this duty. The guidance and more information can be found at: **www.gov.uk/government/publications/prevent-duty-guidance**

An understanding of education illustrates your commitment to a future teaching career. Useful sources of information include the BBC education website and the *Times Educational Supplement*. In addition, refer back to Chapter 2 for lots of information on how to update yourself on current issues in education. Some teacher education programmes will ask you to choose an educational topic and read up about it before the interview. Look at it in depth so you are able to express your point of view clearly – political outlook is unimportant.

How much knowledge do I need about the subject I am applying to teach?

This depends on the course for which you have applied, but the prospectus and entry criteria will give you an idea of this. You should have good starter knowledge at the level you will be teaching – and you will develop this during your course. If applying for primary education, the more knowledge you have about national curriculum areas the better, but no-one is expected to have an in-depth knowledge across the board. Show solid understanding of at least one of the following: mental maths, grammar, spelling and phonics. Good subject knowledge for secondary teaching can be impressive, but this is of course only part of the picture – you need to be able to teach the subject to others.

What type of references do I need?

The most useful references are, for example, from a school or organisation where the applicant has worked recently, or from a university tutor or work manager (full-time/part-time employment).

5.3 What makes a good ITT interview candidate?

If you have prepared a strong ITT application, you will be well on the way to appearing a strong interview candidate – even *before* you arrive at your interview. Keep up the good work on the day of the interview.

To prepare thoroughly for interview, practise making positive statements about yourself, as this will really help to make you fluent with your replies by the time of your interview. Practise answering the type of questions you are likely to be asked at interview. Saying it out loud really will help get you interview-fit.

What should I wear?

Wear what you'd expect a professional attending an interview to wear – better to be overdressed than underdressed. Most institutions will expect *smart* (rather than *smart casual*). And definitely not jeans and a T-shirt – you'll want to be remembered for what you have said in your interview, not what you have worn.

Is it a good idea to bring anything else with me to the interview (apart from what I have been told to bring along with me)?

Interviews are tightly scheduled, so time is going to be limited. It's unlikely that you'll have the chance to discuss items you've not been instructed to bring. But it does make sense to bring pens and pencils if you know you are going to be doing a test or written task.

Who will interview me?

You will probably be interviewed by a combination of course staff and senior staff from their partner schools. The school staff's views will be at least as important as those representing the teacher training institution.

Do I need to know all about schools and education?

No, you can't know everything. But demonstrate that you can reflect intelligently on the experience and knowledge that you do have. Do some homework on the web as well (see Chapter 2), as some background knowledge of current issues in education shows interest and commitment.

How much do I need to know about the subject I am applying to teach – will I be quizzed on this?

That depends on the institution and your chosen course. For secondary education courses (and primary education courses offering a specialism) you may be quizzed on your subject knowledge. For other primary courses, institutions will expect students to be honest about what they consider their strengths and weaknesses across primary subjects.

Do I need to be able to provide specific examples of what I have done in the past?

You will need to be able to talk about and reflect on your own school experiences. Institutions may ask you to illustrate your experience with a specific example. Be ready to speak in depth about what you have seen in the classroom – and what you have learnt from that experience. The interviewers will gain an insight into your ability to work with children and how you reflect on these situations. Ideally you will also show how you successfully foster positive relationships with pupils and staff in schools.

Do I need to be prepared to work with the other candidates – or will the interview be individual?

This will vary, but many institutions expect you to interact through group activities. Be prepared, as some interviews may start as a group interview to see how well you work with others. In such a group context, you should aim to engage actively, taking part without forcing your opinions onto others. Observers will be looking for several things:

- **the ability to get involved (without dominating the group);**
- **playing a full part in the task/discussion;**
- **building constructively on the work or ideas of others;**
- **negotiating while not always just agreeing;**
- **listening to others' points of view.**

TIP: A good tactic is to ask a question that encourages someone to expand on their point. Make eye contact with the person who is speaking and remember to smile.

How much will I be expected to know about the course?

Do your homework and find out what you can about the course from the website and course handbook. Attend open days to find out how the course is structured. Be ready to answer the following questions:

- **Why do you want to study at this institution?**
- **Why have you applied for this particular course?**

Do I need to have wanted to be a teacher for a long time?

No. It is more important to show that you have been into schools to find out what teaching entails – and that you are keen to be a teacher right now. Relevant recent experience will show commitment and suitability for teaching. Enthusiasm, passion and the ability to help pupils develop and grow in their learning is more important than simply stating 'I've always wanted to be a teacher'. Ideally you should be sure what age group you want to teach. Think of your own *angle* or *story* – this is your application. Be honest and be yourself.

Is it OK to say that although I want to teach now, I don't plan to teach until I retire?

This may not be the wisest move. Training costs money, time and effort – and no institution will want to invest in someone who may teach for only a year or two. Although you may even end up changing career at a later date, this will be the earliest stage of your career as a teacher – and you should always present yourself in a positive light at interview.

Will I have to teach pupils during my interview?

Yes, you might. Increasingly, interviewers are looking for evidence of applicants' suitability to teach, and what better way could there be than to ask you to interact with a group of unknown pupils! This could involve reading or telling a story, or leading a simple activity, while you are being observed. Those watching will of course be considering your potential, and will not expect you to function as a qualified teacher. Your pre-existing classroom experience should prepare you well for this.

Don't worry – you've prepared thoroughly for this interview. Now go and show everyone what a good ITT interview candidate you really are!

6 | What is teacher training really like?

This chapter on teacher training is divided into two sections:

6.1 One student's perspective
6.2 ITT tutors' perspective

6.1 One student explains what it's really like as a trainee teacher

From an early age, I always had an interest in education. In fact, it sometimes feels like it is the only thing that I have been any good at in my life – bringing me immense pleasure and enjoyment. This was the main reason for me entering ITT and pursuing a career as a secondary mathematics teacher. I decided that I wanted to inspire children to see the benefits of education.

I found the process of applying to my course fairly straightforward and not particularly daunting. The interview was a different matter, although this may have been because I was only 17 at the time. I did not really know what to expect from the whole process and had not really been given any guidance about the interview. I would have liked to have had a rough outline of what they were going to ask me so that I could have prepared some stronger responses. I accept there has to be an element of unpredictability with interviews, but some general guidance would have really benefited me and allayed some of my worries (see Chapter 5).

Having said that, the interview was not too surprising. I answered the usual questions on my background and why I wanted to pursue a career in teaching, and what I thought the job would entail. However, a couple of the questions really threw me.

How I would teach this topic? What's the point of this subject in real life?

I found this sort of questioning difficult: tough questions which forced me to answer on the spot – and think outside the box.

My chosen university was relatively supportive in providing me with information, such as required reading for the course. Looking back on my three years at university though, I feel that initially I was not fully prepared for the course. For someone embarking on ITT, I would advise them to get some proper teaching experience *before* they start the course so that they can get a taste of what the real thing is like – and so that it will not be a shock to them when they start teaching. Before beginning my course, I got some work experience as a Teaching Assistant in a school for two weeks. Although I enjoyed the experience, I now feel that I should have aimed to get more out of my time in the classroom and really tried to experience what teaching is like. This would have given me a more realistic idea of what to expect later. I was to find the placements on my course particularly challenging. I think if I had experienced more teaching practice *before* the course started, I would have been much better prepared to cope with the demands of my placement. I think perhaps my lack of genuine teaching practice somewhat hindered my development into a confident teacher who had the respect of the class.

I have always cared a lot about what I have achieved in my own education, and for the majority of my course this aspect concerned me the most. Generally, I thought the assignments and academic work were OK. Although for some students it may be quite exciting to write an essay the night before it is due in, for me it made sense to start on essays as early as possible. Before starting the course, I imagined that I would learn more about how to teach particular topics on my ITT course. Instead, I seemed to pick this up as the course progressed and I also learned through experience on placement. As expected, we studied theory in depth, and this proved useful as I began to see the link between theory and practice.

There is no doubt about the importance of academic qualifications. During the first two years of my degree, academic attainment occupied my thoughts a great deal, while in my final year I worried about obtaining Qualified Teacher Status (QTS). At times, I thought that I was never going to do it. I have never been particularly confident and I sometimes wondered whether I was capable of achieving QTS. I built it up in my mind to be always just out of reach. I often doubted my ability to complete the training and, at some points, thought I was never going to get my degree. It became everything to me and dominated my life. In the end, I managed to get a first in my degree, get my dissertation published, and also obtain a 2 (good) in my teaching. I have frequently doubted my teaching ability, but to be graded a good teacher allowed me to break free from those doubts. I do not believe that I necessarily studied any harder than my peers; I would say we were all a hard-working bunch. At the time of training, however, it was frustrating to observe that teaching often seemed more natural to others than it did to me.

The skills tests are hard to quantify in terms of difficulty, although you could possibly say that they are approximately grade C GCSE Maths and English. Some people found them quite easy, others really struggled. I believe that getting used to the format of the tests is the main thing, as there is a certain technique required to pass them. The tests online provided by the government are useful, but I would definitely advise buying a book or workbook to supplement your study. Prepare for the tests as you would for any other exam. Become familiar with all the course content, do some revision and make sure you try out a few practice tests (see Chapters 3 and 4). You may also want to consider getting a tutor. I have witnessed the benefits of this, as I have since tutored many people for the skills tests. It is always good to have someone else to work with: if this is not a tutor, then you may want to find an amenable friend or family member. My university offered free support sessions for this, which is another option.

While my course panned out pretty much as I had expected, I could not have predicted how placements worked. I guess the hardest aspect of the whole course was the teaching in school placements. There was never a dull moment and you certainly had to think on your feet. As a kid I was fairly well behaved at school, but I did see bad behaviour in some pupils. However, I think what surprised me most on placement was the sheer volume of tasks which a trainee teacher has to undertake – planning lessons, admin, teaching, as well as marking. It was certainly a very full-on experience, but I also derived some satisfaction from all the work. One thing is for sure: working in a school is never boring – and it is often a thrilling job.

You cannot change how unpredictable the placements are going to be, because there is always going to be an element of volatility. If you study hard, you can do well in the academic work, but placements are more complex. At first, my placement was quite tough. But the unpredictability also makes the placement exciting. Over time I found my feet and eventually achieved some sort of competency, although as a teacher I am still a long way off being the finished article. The trickiest part of the course was teaching lessons on my placement, but this all got easier with time and practice. You are learning something new every day.

It was really weird to go into a school as a teacher and have pupils call me 'Sir'. It was a good feeling though! I was just surprised at how different this was from attending school as a pupil, and I really gained an insight into what being a teacher is like. Some of my family work in education, so I always had a rough idea, but going into a school and being expected to take charge of a class suddenly made it real. On my placements, though, I felt similar to how I did on work experience: I did not really feel like I quite belonged. This appears to be something which many student teachers experience.

The quality and personality of the teachers varied in each school that I worked in, and this variety makes working in a school much more interesting. Most of the teachers were helpful and supportive and, over the course of my three years' training, no one really caused me any problems. However, teachers tend to be busy, so often I simply had to learn things for myself, which helped me develop essential skills of independence and problem-solving. Teachers tend to be very close in their departments, which makes for a productive working environment.

Managing a class of children was difficult, irrespective of the class size. At first, standing at the front of the class was nerve-wracking. I have always had problems with my confidence, and here I was thrown out of my comfort zone. I had always been a follower in life, while secretly I craved to be a leader. Becoming a teacher gave me the chance to be in charge for once, rather than being told what to do! This was a very liberating experience and something which I came to enjoy.

Planning a lesson was quite simple, although I think that there is an unnecessary amount of paperwork in schools. It was pretty time-consuming having to prepare for every lesson. However, this was also a valuable learning experience for me, as was marking. I soon discovered the best times to do marking and lesson planning – straight after school so that I could try to have some time to myself in the evenings. Remembering to find time for yourself is very important when you are training to be a teacher.

I enjoyed explaining concepts and ideas to the pupils the most, as well as going around and helping them while they were doing their work. I also liked talking to them during form time and extra-curricular activities – this helped me to get to know them on a different level (while not having to discipline them all the time). Knowing the pupils better made teaching them much easier. I am an extrovert who likes talking to people, and as I expected, these were the parts of the placement that I enjoyed the most.

The personality and teaching style that you develop as a teacher is important. I would advise students not to be scared to become their own type of teacher: it helps to have a vision of the teacher you want to be, and not to let anyone change that. All too often teachers are encouraged to be too similar. It is important to develop your own style and identity. Some people might say that certain types of people cannot be a teacher, but I would disagree: anyone can be a teacher if they put their mind to it. The reality is that it takes some people longer than others. There were a few people who dropped out of my course but quite a few of them transferred to a primary teaching course. What helps people succeed is determination. You are going to have to show resilience at some stage.

I believe the ITT course provides a wonderful learning experience. It certainly makes you ready to become a teacher, particularly if you prepare well from the start for placement. The course can also give you so much more: I think I have definitely grown as a person as a result. Plenty of people thought that I would never get through teacher training. But I did, and I have more confidence now than ever before. I can pursue new goals in my life. Having qualified as a teacher, I am finally starting to get rid of my own doubts. If I had not gone on teacher training, none of this would have been possible.

6.2 Some insight from a conversation with a group of ITT tutors at the University of Exeter

This is not an exhaustive description of teacher training. The conversation was based on a series of questions designed to get some insight into what training is really like.

The role of the teacher

Classroom persona is really important. A trainee teacher should assume the role of a teacher – and begin to embody it, really. The change of viewpoint can challenge those who have previously worked in schools in a different role, such as teaching assistants (TAs). They not only have to take on a new teacher persona, but they must step away from the TA persona too.

Prospective trainees should make the most of any pre-course school experiences: both the time in school that they organise themselves before they apply, and the time that they spend in school before they start the course. Learn from early teaching experiences. Really think about what you observe in the classroom and consider what you want and need to get out of it. The real 'work' of teacher training starts here: listen, watch and keep alert and curious. Try to see the learning that is happening and ask how you can tell that learning is taking place. Did the children learn from the lesson? Ensure you are open-minded. Are you ready for the experience to change your view of teaching? Make sure that when you go into the classroom you are prepared to look at the teaching, specifically. Be prepared to look at the learning first and then evaluate the teaching (the teaching can only be good if the learning is good).

When you teach, there is an element of acting, or performing. Act and look like a teacher – dress like a teacher, too. You should, of course, maintain a 'difference' between yourself and the class. You are there as a teacher, not a friend. Remain professional throughout and always have your teacher's hat on.

Do not repeat the past

While it may seem quite tempting to some prospective trainees to go back to their old school to do pre-course experience, you should think twice about this. ITT providers will be much more impressed if you go somewhere new. You will also learn more. You will have a clearer view of who you are in the new school – and not be treated as an ex-pupil. You will be able to consider schools and education with a fresh perspective.

Behaviour

Managing behaviour at school should not be seen in isolation, because it is all inter-twined with planning good lessons and delivering well-paced learning. Behaviour in the classroom tends to be more of an anxiety than a huge problem to tackle. Trainees often worry about it, perhaps after reading articles in the press about really bad behaviour in some schools. You will need to learn quickly that a 'well-behaved' class is not a silent, obedient one. Everything is a little more complicated than that. Good learning behaviour includes a lot of oral interaction, often between groups of learners.

You are accountable, first and foremost, for the pupils' learning. A teacher is accountable for the overall learning of all pupils, not just the behaviour and day-to-day work of one or two individuals, which might be what the TA is responsible for. In this way, the difference between a TA and a teacher is clear. Classroom teaching is different from one-on-one: it is about realising the needs of the individual and the class as a group all the time. Try to see the bigger picture – you are helping with the learning of the whole class over a whole year – and not just a single lesson.

In reality, there is no big secret to managing behaviour. If you plan good lessons, and have a clear structure and a strong positive presence, the behaviour will often fall into place. The majority of trainees 'crack' behaviour in the first few weeks of the course – or are clearly en route towards 'cracking it' at that early stage.

Trying to maintain good behaviour in class is one worry, but trainees soon realise that the bigger challenge is to keep the children's attention and focus on lessons. The world today is full of swift, slick information and entertainment delivery – children are used to, and expect, that now. There will frequently be one or two students with behaviour issues that trainees (and teachers, for that matter) cannot resolve with a 'quick fix'. 'Behaviour' is not really about them alone – it is about the whole class, and the context (environment, con-tent, teaching and learning resources, teaching and learning activities, support).

Reflective practice

All teachers have bad lessons that just do not go right. This can happen, and always will. You need to pick yourself up, reflect on what went wrong – and move on, quickly. The key is to look back on lessons and really try to pin down why something went wrong (if it did) so that you can fix the problem for the next time. In the end, teaching is a learning expe-rience, both for the learners, and for you as a trainee teacher.

Perfection is just not possible. Some trainees will be high achievers who find it difficult to cope with this idea. A perfectionist streak does not really help in teacher training. You must learn and improve as a teacher, but be realistic about what you can achieve in your lessons. Often students who are too concerned with perfection become derailed when some problems arise – or they find it really difficult to be the 'teacher' in the room. If you *are* a perfectionist, learn from your experiences and mistakes. Embrace them. Use them as handy indicators to improve your teaching. You are at the beginning of a process. Do not worry: it all takes time and you will need to stick at it.

Teaching practice *will* feel uncomfortable at times. And you will learn things about your-self that you may not like. You need to be ready and willing to take this on. Teaching may feel like holding up a mirror to yourself. The vast majority of trainees appear to be really self-critical. Do not make the mistake of looking outside yourself for fault. Try to keep a sense of proportion when thinking about things that may have gone wrong. No one will go through teaching practice without 'a bad day', but if you do experience one, be prepared to learn from it as much as you can. And move on.

Trainees often need reassurance that they will get plenty of help and support while they are still learning. Some 'deep end' models of teacher training exist, but most trainees receive good support so they can work through all the challenges. Trainees should think hard about how much support they would like or need. Look carefully at what different courses offer. You can ask more questions to find this out. There are a number of routes available into teaching, but the structure of courses can vary from place to place – and this includes how much support you get, too. Sometimes, prospective trainees can struggle to understand how their courses will work, so it really does pay to take time to find this out. Proper research into the courses you apply to will help you make the right choice for *you*.

Applicants need to prepare well, but they should also realise that tutors are constantly assessing them. Some trainees may even have to teach as part of their interviews. If this is the case, keep in mind that perfection is not a realistic goal. If all trainees could teach fabulously from the start, they would have no need for training!

Always be realistic

When applying, find out how many places each provider has to offer. If the provider has only one place for your particular subject, an impressive second place means that you still will not be offered a place. If, however, a provider has ten places to offer, your chances should improve dramatically. Be aware of your own value. Look at your choices, and see the whole 'market' of teacher training – and how ITT providers and trainees fit into this. A thoughtful and intelligent approach will work best.

Academic assignments

All courses (including School Direct) will have an academic element. If you have not written an academic piece like an essay for a long time, you will have to prepare for this, because you will need to write two long social science essays for most courses. Do not worry, you are not alone: many trainees who have written essays more recently than you may also fear their academic assignments. Trainees should not, however, become overwrought about 'academic' work. It does not have to be daunting at all. Preparation is key and, often, the hardest part is making a start with the writing. Remember you should not be stuffing your essay with as many difficult words as possible to impress your tutors. Think clearly, write clearly. And, when you are editing your essay, read your work out loud.

Specialisms

Your subject or specialism is important (some primary trainees have this too). You should embrace this and get the most you can from it. A specific focus on a subject can really add an extra string to your bow when you enter the world of teaching. Always try to use it to your advantage.

Working with others

The vast majority of the time, working with other teachers in schools is really positive. Mentors and other members of staff will be keen to help. Mentors can be pushed for time, however, so trainees should always be sensitive to this. You always need to be professional about your relationship with your mentor too. Being over-friendly can sometimes be as detrimental as not really getting on with a mentor at all. A trainee is there to learn and that should be the focus, first and foremost.

State schools in England have their own unique 'culture'. If you have no first-hand experience of this – for example, you were educated privately or in another country – you should take time to find out more about it. The British Council has some information on the UK state education system that might be of use to trainees or candidates for whom this applies.

Getting the most out of training

Trainee teachers say they enjoy teaching and get a huge amount out of working with pupils. They enjoy having a peer group during training. Everyone benefits from the friendships they build during training – sharing ideas and learning from their own and each other's successes and mistakes.

Teacher training is a journey. You will really gain from the experience if you are ready to learn new things. Be prepared to open your mind to what you see and do. You will probably find that you change as a person, too. By the end of the course, most trainees are very different people. Group photographs before and after training show that the students hold themselves in a different way. It is not helpful for tutors to think of it as throwing trainees in at the deep end and seeing if they survive. The process is more about supporting you and gradually giving you more and more responsibility as you go. As a trainee teacher, always be open-minded. Be prepared to learn new things that you never even considered about schools, education, children – and yourself.

Dropping out

There is no single reason why trainees drop out. Generally speaking, though, it is a case of life getting in the way. Drop outs are perhaps not as high as is believed. Although the following article is not current, you may find it of interest as part of the bigger picture.

www.tes.co.uk/article.aspx?storycode=2444282

Challenges

The most challenging part of the course is often the workload – and the sheer range of skills trainees are developing *at the same time*. Becoming a teacher is an identity shift for many and you are sure to change during the course of the year, especially if you have recently graduated. Prepare yourself for the pastoral role of teachers: you may soon be exposed to issues that you have just never had to think about before. Although you may start your course with a very clear focus on teaching your subject, it is so much more than that. You may be surprised by the pupils, their variety, their needs and all the things that you will need to discover about yourself, too.

Literacy Glossary

*Abbreviation A shortened form of a word or phrase; usually, but not always, consisting of a letter or group of letters taken from the word or phrase. For example, the word *approximately* can be replaced by the abbreviation 'approx'.

Accent An accent is the distinctive system of pronunciation that listeners identify as being used by a regional or social group. Accents are neither easy nor hard to follow, merely familiar or unfamiliar.

*Acronym An abbreviation made from the initial letters of a group of words and often pronounced as a single word, for example, RAM (random access memory).

Adjective An adjective is a word, phrase or clause that tells us about a noun: *clever child, tense student, concerned teacher*; *a lesson about Spain*; *the teacher who had done supply work there previously*. The clause comes after the noun whereas the phrase may come before (*the predictably over-anxious child from Ashton*) as well as more typically, afterwards.

Adverb Adverbs tell us when, where or how something took place. They usually modify verbs but can also modify adjectives, other adverbs or sentences: *Joe sang happily*; *Annie is a very engaged reader*; *Alice danced very gracefully*; *Lucy had, fortunately, brought her trumpet with her.*

Not all adverbs end in *ly*. *Fast* is usually used as an adverb. *Very*, used above, is an adverb that appears only as an intensifier of some other word.

Adverbial clause An adverbial clause does the work of an adverb: it tells us when, where or how something took place: *The head came into the hall when all the children were there*; *Ann did her print-making where she usually worked*; *Pam ran down the corridor as if she was being chased.*

Adverbial phrase An adverbial phrase also does the work of an adverb. It is a group of words based on an adverb but coming before or after it or both: *very quickly, talked as volubly as the deputy*. An adverb can be substituted for an adverbial phrase.

Agree/agreement If one person does something, the verb should be in its singular form: *Annie sings*. If more than one does something, the verb should be in its plural form: *Joe and Sally are painting.*

*Analogy Drawing a comparison to show a similarity; for example, if you were describing the flow of electricity, you might choose to use the flow of water as an analogy.

*Apostrophe A **punctuation mark** used for two purposes:

- to show that something belongs to someone (the *possessive* form); for example, *the pupil's work*, or
- to show that letters have been missed out (a *contraction*); for example, *you've* is the shortened form of *you have*.

Attachment ambiguity Ambiguity may arise when it is unclear if a phrase should be attached to this or that other phrase. In *The teacher told the class what had happened to the caretaker on the stairs*, it is possible to understand that *on the stairs* was where something happened to the caretaker but also that it was *on the stairs* that the teacher told the class.

*Audio Of, or relating to, sound.

Brackets: see **punctuation: parentheses.**

British English This term is normally used to describe the features common to English English, Welsh English, Scottish English, and Hiberno-English.

Bullet points Bullets should only be used to aid comprehension by highlighting key points and breaking up long passages of text. Overuse can be distracting and make text harder to digest. Ideally bullet points should lead out from a 'platform' or 'stem' statement and complete a grammatically correct sentence. However, there are no hard and fast rules on this. Often what is acceptable is governed by a preferred 'house-style'.

Capital letters: see **punctuation.** Use capitals for proper nouns, acronyms and the beginning of sentences. Note that upper case in an acronym does not necessarily denote upper case in the full description, e.g. EPQ/extended project qualification; PGCE/post-graduate certificate in education.

Clause A group of words with a finite verb (it would be a phrase if it did not have a finite verb). As it is finite, the verb typically has a subject. A clause may be a sentence: *Alice laughed.* A sentence may contain several clauses: *Alice laughed and Lucy giggled* links two clauses of equal significance with the conjunction *and*; this is a co-ordinate sentence. *Alice laughed because Lucy giggled* links two clauses that differ in significance; this is a complex sentence in which a main clause – *Alice laughed* – is linked to a subordinate clause that is not independent of other clauses but exists to explain the main clause on which it depends.

Coherence/cohesion A well-made text feels coherent. What holds it together is the writer's use of cohesion: cohesive devices that relate parts of the text to each other. Adverbs between sentences are such devices: *The IT suite was heavily used.* **However,** *rising numbers were putting pressure on its use.*

Repetition of a word or some reference to it is another device. Perhaps the one we are most aware of is the use of a pronoun to refer to its noun. A noun may refer back to its noun: *The Ofsted report was scrutinised by the Governors before* **it** *was presented to parents. Although* **some** *were apprehensive, most of the class looked forward to the cliff-walk.*

*Colloquial A colloquialism is a term used in everyday language rather than in formal speech or writing; for example, the use of the word *kids* rather than *children* in the following sentence:

The kids in Years 4 and 5 are having a swimming gala next week.

*Colon: see **punctuation**.

*Comma: see **punctuation**.

*Compound word A word made when two words are joined to form a new word; for example, *foot/ball*, *foot/fall*. Sometimes, a hyphen is used between the two parts of the word, as in *over-anxious*.

*Conjunctions (see also connectives) These are words such as *and*, *but* and *or*, that are used to join words, phrases or clauses. There are two kinds of conjunction:

- **Co-ordinating conjunctions** (*and*, *but*, *or* and *so*).These link items that have equal status grammatically, for example:

  *We could fly to Paris **or** we could take the train.*
  *He plans to fly to Dublin **but** he will arrive there very early.*

- **Subordinating conjunctions** (*when, while, before, after, since, until, if, because, although, that*). If the two items do not have equal status, a subordinating conjunction is used. Most commonly, this happens when a main clause is joined to a subordinate clause, for example:
- *I was late for the meeting **because** the train was delayed.*

Connective Connectives connect words, phrases, clauses and sentences. Those that operate *within* the sentence, that connect words, phrases and clauses, are called conjunctions: *and, but, if, or, because, although*, etc. Those that connect sentences (*Pam and Tom worked very hard all term. **Luckily,** their efforts paid off*) include some conjunctions but also adverbs such as: *On the other hand, Later, While we were singing*, etc.

Consistency A good style is, among other things, consistent. The writer will always spell *judgement* with that first *e* or always without it. Punctuation demands a very consistent style, as when adverbs such as *however* always appear between commas if they occur in the middle of a sentence.

*Consonant Consonants are letters and speech sounds that are not vowels. See **vowel**.

Contraction If we try to write down informal speech, we will sometimes need contractions. These help us to write some contracted combinations of words: *do not* becomes *don't, will not* becomes *won't*. The words are contracted by omitting some letters and inserting an apostrophe into the space that is left. Occasionally, as with *won't*, there is also a change in spelling.

*Contradict, contradicted, contradiction To contradict is to state that something is the opposite of what has been said; a contradiction is a statement that contradicts.

Convention While the rules of grammar, like the laws of gravity, get their authority by describing how things are, there are some practices that are matters of social convention and have no other explanation. The conventions governing spelling and punctuation, for example, have changed over time.

*Dash Use a dash, rather than a hyphen, to represent ranges of numbers, e.g. 11–16 years.

A pair of dashes can be used to separate an interruption within a sentence, e.g. 'Most pupils – especially in extended schools – enjoy after school activities'. If the interruption comes at the end of the sentence, only one dash is used.

*Definite article The; see **determiner**.

*Department for Education In full at first mention, then the DfE.

*Determiner These are words used with nouns to help define them, for example, *this* computer, *a* pencil, *the* book, and limit, i.e. determine the reference of the noun in some way. Determiners include:

- articles (*a/an, the*)
- demonstratives (*this/that, these/those*)
- possessives (*my/your/his/her/its/our/their*)
- quantifiers (*some, any, no, many, few, all, either, each,* etc.)
- numbers (*one, two, three,* etc.), and
- some question words (*which, what, whose*).

Words that are used as determiners are followed by a noun (though not necessarily immediately). For example, *this* book is yours; *this* black book is yours; *which* book is yours?

Many determiners can also be used as **pronouns**. These include demonstrative pronouns, question words, numbers and most quantifiers. When used as pronouns, determiners are not followed by a noun; they refer to the noun: *this* is for you (where *this* refers to *this school, this book,* etc.).

Dialect A variety of a language that is spoken by a specific group or in a specific area of the country and whose words and grammar show some differences from those used in other dialects of English. The prestige of a dialect derives from the prestige of its speakers, not from its linguistic features. *Accent* is usually taken to be related but different because it focuses on the *substance* of the language: in the case of an accent, that substance is the sound of speech.

*Dialogue A conversation between two or more people.

Digraph Two letters that represent one sound: *ch* and *ck* in *check*; *sh* in *show*; *ph* in *phonically*.

*Discourse marker A word or phrase (such as *however, nevertheless, well, OK,* or *right!*) that is used to signal a pause or change of direction in conversation.

Ellipsis If a sentence can be understood when a word or a group of words is removed, the parts deleted have been ellipted. One of the commonest examples of ellipsis is the dropping of the relative pronoun *that*: *The school [that] I like best.* A more sophisticated usage is: *My class, if lively, is still well behaved. If lively* here is an ellipted version of something like *even if it is lively.*

*Evaluate To assess; when asked to evaluate whether a statement is supported or implied by a text, you are being asked to judge how clearly the text does or does not spell out the information given in the statement.

*Fewer/less Use 'fewer' for things you can count (e.g. books, pupils) and 'less' for things you can't count (e.g. space, scope).

Grammar Grammar, or syntax, is usually used to mean how sentences are organised. It can, however, also refer to the organisation of larger units: the text level. *Cohesion* is the study of the grammar of these larger units. *Morphology* is the branch of grammar that deals with word-formation.

*Hyphens Use hyphens for compound adjectives, e.g. the up-to-date situation but keep the directory up to date, a long-term plan but in the long term. Do not use a hyphen between an adverb and the adjective or the verb it modifies, e.g. a hotly disputed penalty, a constantly evolving policy.

*Imply, implied, implicit Something implied is hinted at without being stated explicitly. It is implicit.

*Indefinite article *A* or *an*; see **determiner**.

Infinitive The (non-finite) form of a verb that opens with *to*: *to learn*, *to study*, *to think*.

Morpheme The smallest bit of language that has meaning. A morpheme may be a whole word (*cabbage*) or a word may have several morphemes (*un + help + ful*, *govern + or*, *head + teach + er*). **Suffixes** and **prefixes** are all morphemes.

Morphology see **grammar**.

Noun Nouns refer to objects, ideas, things, places. They take a plural form (usually, add *s*).

Some nouns, however, do not normally take a plural form: *happiness*. They have a possessive form (add *'s* or *s'*). They can be substituted by a pronoun, take a word like *the*, *this*, *a* before them and take a verb after them.

- **Noun phrase:** a group of words that works as a noun. A pronoun could be substituted for it: *The first person to have been Chair of the Education Committee.*
- **Noun clause:** a group of words that has a finite verb and that acts as a noun. Here, the clause acts as the subject: ***That I was late with my reports yet again was hard to swallow.*** Here, it acts as the object: *The class was desperate to know **if the school trip was still on.***
- **Collective nouns** refer to a group of things or people: *collection, family, group, class, set*. It is usually safest to treat collective nouns as singular unless the meaning is that they should be read as plural.
- **Proper nouns** refer to specific people, places, organisations, etc., and have a capital initial letter: *Dot, Mike*; *Salford, Canterbury*; *Training and Development Agency*.

Paragraph One or more sentences grouped together because they are about the same topic or because they form one utterance in a dialogue. It is separated from the adjacent paragraphs by beginning on a new line.

Parenthesis A word or phrase that interrupts the sentence is marked at both boundaries by parentheses: brackets, commas or dashes:

> *The Irwell (which flows through Salford) was the focus of their local studies.*
> *The Irwell – which flows through Salford – was the focus of their local studies.*
> *The Irwell, which flows through Salford, was the focus of their local studies.*

Participle The present participle is a form of the verb that ends in *ing*: *learning, reading, writing*; the past participle is a form of the verb that ends, normally, in *ed*: *talked, walked, displayed*. However, there are irregular verbs that have other endings: *bought, written, sung*, etc.

The present participle is used to construct continuous tenses: *she **was teaching**, she **is teaching**, she **will be teaching**.* It sometimes works as a noun (it can then be called a gerund): *learning is good.*

The past participle follows an auxiliary verb to form the perfect past tense: *I **have taught**, they **have learned**.* The passive voice uses an auxiliary with a past participle: *the class **was cheated out** of their expected success, the in-service day **was cancelled**.*

Both participles can be used as adjectives: *broken, breaking, entangled.*

Phoneme A single speech sound. We use 44–48 different phonemes when we speak English, depending on the accent we use. Spelling tries to represent phonemes but tries to do other things as well that may conflict with that attempt. The letters *th* in *this* represent one phoneme but in *thing* they represent a different phoneme.

Phonetics Phonetics is a way of describing the sounds we use in speech. It has nothing to do with phonics.

Phrase A group of words without a verb (it would be a clause if it had a finite verb). Phrases can be **nouns**: *the twentieth position in the class*; **adjectives**: *very clever*; **adverbs**: *too early*; or **verbs**: *was practising.*

Plural The plural form of a noun shows that more than one thing is being referred to. Plural nouns typically end in *s* (*book + s = books; girl + s = girls*), *es* (*box + es = boxes, circus + es = circuses*) or *ies* (*fairy* becomes *fairies, story* becomes *stories*). There are also some irregular plurals, such as *children, women, men, geese, sheep.*

Possessive Possessive pronouns – *my/mine*, etc. – show who or what owns what: *my whiteboard, its cursor.* In writing, nouns show possession by adding an apostrophe and, as appropriate, the letter *s.*

Predicate The part of a sentence that is not the subject; it is about the subject: *The headteacher **arrived too early**.*

Prefix A **morpheme** that is added at the beginning of a word: *a* in *atheist*, *un* in *unhelpful*.

Preposition Prepositions usually link a noun or noun phrase with another one or with a verb. Prepositions such as *at, on, in, over, by, with, near, through* are used to introduce adjective phrases in *The display **over** the radiator* or *That boy **by** the boundary fence* and to introduce adverb phrases in *Joe is **on** the go as usual* and *Annie's balloon rose **into** the sky.*

Pronoun A word used instead of a noun, a noun phrase or a group of nouns. It may be a **personal pronoun**: *I/me, you/you, he/him, she/her, it/it, we/us, they/them*; a **possessive pronoun**: *my/mine, your/yours, his/his, her/hers, our/ours, their/theirs, its/its*; a **reflexive pronoun**: *myself, herself, themselves*; or an **interrogative pronoun** (used in questions): *who/whom, whose, which, what*.

Punctuation The standard set of marks used in written and printed texts to clarify meaning and to separate sentences, words and parts of words. The most commonly used punctuation marks in English are:

- **apostrophe** (')
- **colon** (:)
- **comma** (,)
- **exclamation mark** (!)
- **full stop** (.)
- **hyphen** (-)
- **inverted commas** (see *speech marks*)
- **parentheses** (singular: *parenthesis,* also known as brackets or ellipses (singular, ellipsis) (())
- **question mark** (?)
- **semi-colon** (;)
- **speech marks,** also known as quotation marks or inverted commas (" " or ' ').

    Also included are special signals such as:

- the use of a space before and after a block or words to indicate the start of a new **paragraph**
- the convention of using an upper case (or capital) letter to begin a proper name or a new sentence.

***Redundancy** Redundancy is the use of duplicative, unnecessary or useless wording, also known as **tautology**.

Relative clause Relative clauses come after nouns and function as adjectives. Typically, they open with a relative pronoun: *who, whom, that, which, whose*: *The teacher **that we hoped to appoint** was not as experienced as two other candidates.* Note that, in this case, the relative pronoun, *that*, can be deleted without losing the meaning.

Sentence A sentence is a clause or a group of clauses. Each clause needs to have a finite verb.

- **Finite verbs** are ones that tell us about tense; they almost invariably have a subject: *Ann and Tony both found maths easy*.
- **Non-finite verb** forms are the infinitive – *to teach* – and the participles that end in *-ed* or *-ing*.
- Sentences can be declarative: *The class rushed into the hall*; **interrogative**: *Can't your class do anything quietly?*; **imperative**: *Slow down*! or **exclamative**: *That's great*!

*Sentence stem In the test items, this is the first part of a sentence that requires completion by choosing from several possible endings, for example:
There were four kinds of meetings that day: ... followed by a list.

Singular Nouns can be singular or plural: *book* or *books*; *woman* or *women*. Verbs can also show singularity – *I teach, she teaches* – or plurality – *we teach, they teach*.

STA The Standards and Testing Agency is an executive agency of the Department for Education. The STA is responsible for the development and delivery of all statutory assessments from Early Years to the end of Key Stage 3. This work was previously carried out by the Qualifications and Curriculum Development Agency.

*Standard English The variety of English used in public communication, particularly in writing.

*Statement A sentence that contains a fact or proposition, for example, *this is a glossary*.

Subject A sentence has a subject (a noun or a pronoun) that does something (the verb): *She taught sentence structure very clearly*.

Suffix A **morpheme** that is added at the end of a word: *ed* in *walked*, *ful* in *helpful*.

Syntax Grammar: how sentences are organised.

Tautology The unnecessary repetition of the same idea in different words: in *The Governors met together*, the last word is unnecessary.

*Unit of meaning An identifiably discrete idea.

Verb Words that say what we do or are: *The teacher **stopped** the class because one child **was being** silly*.

- **Active verbs** (verbs in the active voice) tell us what someone did: *Lucy **thanked** the teacher*. **Passive verbs** (verbs in the passive voice) tell us what was done to somebody: *The teacher **was thanked** by Lucy*.
- **Auxiliary verbs** – the main ones are *be, have, do* – accompany main verbs to show tense: *They **have** painted, they **do** run*. Some, called **modal verbs**, express possibility or obligation: *can, could, may, might, will, would, shall, should, must, ought to*.

- **Tense** is the way that a verb tells us when something happened. This is shown in the different forms of the verb, from the past – *learned, has learned, had learned* – to the present – *learns, is learning, does learn* – to the future – *will learn, will have learned*, etc.
- **Number** is the way that a verb shows if one or more than one **subject** did something: *Alice sings, Annie and Joe sing*.

*Vowel The letters a, e, i, o, u; see also **consonant**.

Note

Entries marked with * have been reproduced by courtesy of the TA © Teaching Agency. Permission to reproduce TA copyright material does not extend to any material that is identified as being the copyright of a third party nor to any photographs.

Numeracy Glossary

Accuracy The degree of precision given in the question or required in the answer. For example, a length might be measured to the nearest centimetre. A pupil's reading age is usually given to the nearest month, whilst an average (mean) test result might be rounded to one decimal place.

Bar chart A chart where the number associated with each item is shown either as a horizontal or a vertical bar and where the length of the bar is proportional to the number it represents. The length of the bar is used to show the number of times the item occurs, or the value of the item being measured.

Bar chart showing number of pupils achieving each level

Bar chart arranged horizontally showing mean test scores for four classes

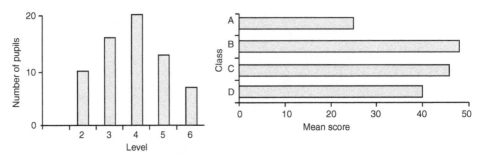

Box and whisker diagram Diagram showing the range and quartile values for a set of data.

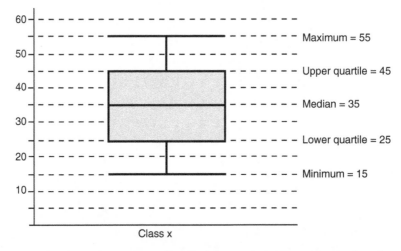

Cohort A group having a common quality or characteristic. For example, 'pupils studying GCSE German this year have achieved higher grades than last year's cohort' (pupils studying GCSE German last year).

Consistent Following the same pattern or style over time with little change. For example, a pupil achieved marks of 84%, 82%, 88% and 85% in a series of mock GCSE tests; her performance was judged to be consistently at the level needed to obtain GCSE grade A*.

Conversion The process of exchanging one set of units for another. Measurement and currency, for example, can be converted from one unit to another, e.g. centimetres to metres, pounds to euros. Conversion of one unit to the other is usually done by using a rule (e.g. 'multiply by $\frac{5}{8}$ to change kilometres into miles'), a formula (e.g. $F = \frac{9}{5} C + 32$, for converting degrees Celsius to degrees Fahrenheit), or a conversion graph.

Correlation The extent to which two quantities are related. For example, there is a positive correlation between two tests, A and B, if a person with a high mark in test A is likely to have a high mark in test B and a person with a low mark in test A is likely to get a low mark in test B. A scatter graph of the two variables may help when considering whether a correlation exists between the two variables.

Cumulative frequency graph A graph in which the frequency of an event is added to the frequency of those that have preceded it. This type of graph is often used to answer a question such as, 'How many pupils are under nine years of age in a local education authority (LA)?' or 'What percentage of pupils gained at least the pass mark of 65 on a test?'.

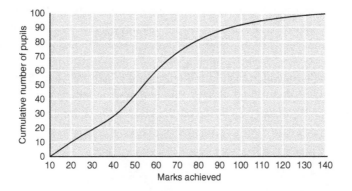

The graph shows the marks pupils achieved. Two pupils scored 10 marks or less, 30 pupils scored 42 marks or less, 60 pupils scored 60 marks or less and 90 pupils scored 95 marks or less. If these were results from a test with a pass mark of 65 marks, then from the graph we can see that 63% of pupils gained 64 marks or less, and so failed the test.

Decimal Numbers based on or counted in a place value system of tens. Normally we talk about decimals when dealing with tenths, hundredths and other decimal fractions less than 1. A decimal point is placed after the units digit in writing a decimal number, e.g. 1.25. The number of digits to the right of the decimal point up to and including the final nonzero digit is expressed as the number of decimal places. In the example above there are two digits after the decimal point, and the number is said to have two decimal places, sometimes expressed as 2 dp. Many simple fractions cannot be expressed exactly as a decimal. For example, the fraction $\frac{1}{3}$ as a decimal is 0.3333... which is usually represented as 0.3 recurring. Decimals are usually rounded to a specified degree of accuracy, e.g. 0.6778 is 0.68 when rounded to 2 dp. 0.5 is always rounded up, so 0.5 to the nearest whole number is 1.

Distribution The spread of a set of statistical information. For example, the number of absentees on a given day in a school is distributed as follows: Monday – 5, Tuesday –17, Wednesday – 23, Thursday – 12 and Friday – 3. A distribution can also be displayed graphically.

Formula A relationship between numbers or quantities expressed using a rule or an equation. For example, final mark = (0.6 x mark 1) + (0.4 x mark 2).

Fraction Fractions are used to express parts of a whole, e.g. $\frac{3}{4}$. The number below the division line, the denominator, records the number of equal parts into which the number above the division line, the numerator, has been divided.

Frequency The number of times an event or quantity occurs.

Greater than A comparison between two quantities. The symbol > is used to represent 'greater than', e.g. 7>2, or >5%.

Interquartile range The numerical difference between the upper quartile and the lower quartile. The lower quartile of a set of data has one quarter of the data below it and three-quarters above it. The upper quartile has three quarters of the data below it and one quarter above it. The inter-quartile range represents the middle 50% of the data.

Line graphs A graph on which the plotted points are joined by a line. It is a visual representation of two sets of related data. The line may be straight or curved. It is often used to show a trend, such as how a particular value is changing over time.

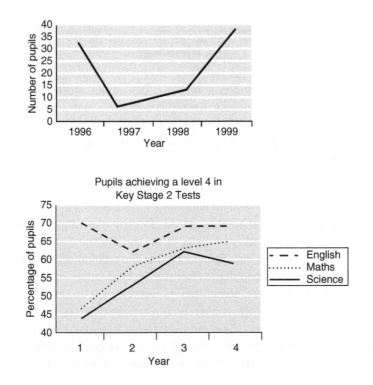

Mean One measure of the 'average' of a set of data. The 'mean' average is usually used when the data involved is fairly evenly spread. For example, the individual costs of four textbooks are £9.95, £8.34, £11.65 and £10.50. The mean cost of a textbook is found by totalling the four amounts, giving £40.44, and then dividing by 4, which gives £10.11. The word average is frequently used in place of the mean, but this can be confusing as both median and mode are also ways of expressing an average.

Median Another measure of the 'average' of a set of data. It is the middle number of a series of numbers or quantities when arranged in order, e.g. from smallest to largest. For example, in the following series of number: 2, 4, 5, 7, 8, 15 and 18, the median is 7. When there is an even number of numbers, the median is found by adding the two middle numbers and then halving the total. For example, in the following series of numbers, 12, 15, 23, 30, 31 and 45, the median is $(23 + 30) \div 2 = 26.5$.

Median and quartile lines Quartiles can be found by taking a set of data that has been arranged in increasing order and dividing it into four equal parts. The first quartile is the value of the data at the end of the first quarter. The median quartile is the value of the data at the end of the second quarter. The third quartile is the value of the data at the end of the third quarter.

Quartile lines can be used to show pupils' progression from one key stage to another, when compared with national or local data:

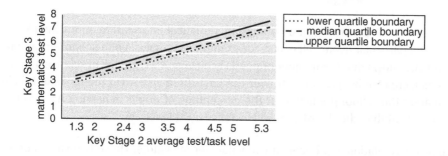

Mode Another measure of the 'average' of a set of data. It is the most frequently occurring result in any group of data. For example, in the following set of exam results: 30%, 34%, 36% 31%, 31%, 30%, 34%, 33%, 31% and 32%, the mode is 31% because this value appears most frequently in the set of results.

Operations The means of combining two numbers or sets of numbers. For example, addition, subtraction, multiplication and division.

Percentage A fraction with a denominator of 100, but written as the numerator followed by '%', e.g. $\frac{30}{100}$ or 30%. A fraction that is not in hundredths can be converted so that the denominator is 100, e.g. $\frac{650}{1000} = \frac{65}{100} = 65\%$. Percentages can be used to compare different fractional quantities. For example, in class A, 10 pupils out of 25 are studying French; in class B, 12 out of 30 pupils are studying French. However, both $\frac{10}{25}$ and $\frac{12}{30}$ are equivalent to $\frac{4}{10}$, or 40%. The same percentage of pupils, therefore, study French in both these classes.

Percentage points The difference between two values, given as percentages. For example, a school has 80% attendance one year and 83% the next year. There has been an increase of 3 percentage points in attendance.

Percentile The values of a set of data that has been arranged in order and divided into 100 equal parts. For example, a year group took a test and the 60th percentile was at a mark of 71. This means that 60% of the cohort scored 71 marks or less. The 25th percentile is the value of the data such that 25% or one quarter of the data is below it and so is the same as the lower quartile. Similarly, the 75th percentile is the same as the upper quartile and the median is the same as the 50th percentile.

Pie chart A pie chart represents the 360° of a circle and is divided into sectors by straight lines from its centre to its circumference. Each sector angle represents a specific proportion of the whole. Pie charts are used to display the relationship of each type or class of data within a whole set of data in a visual form.

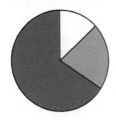

Pie chart showing the distribution of how the total number of pupils in a school take lunch

☐ Packed lunch
▨ Go home
■ School lunch

Prediction A statement based on analysing statistical information about the likelihood that a particular event will occur. For example, an analysis of a school's examination results shows that the number of pupils achieving A*–C grades in science at a school has increased by 3% per year over the past three years. On the basis of this information the school predicts that the percentage of pupils achieving A*–C grades in science at the school next year will increase by at least 2%.

Proportion A relationship between two values or measures. These two values or measures represent the relationship between some part of a whole and the whole itself. For example, a year group of 100 pupils contains 60 boys and 40 girls, so the proportion of boys in the school is 60 out of 100 or 3 out of 5. This is usually expressed as a fraction, in this case, $\frac{3}{5}$.

Quartile (lower) The value of a set of data at the first quarter, 25%, when all the data has been arranged in ascending order. It is the median value of the lower half of all the values in the data set. For example, the results of a test were: 1, 3, 5, 6, 7, 9, 11, 15, 18, 21, 23 and 25. The median is 10. The values in the lower half are 1, 3, 5, 6, 7 and 9. The lower quartile is 5.5. This means that one quarter of the cohort scored 5.5 or less. The lower quartile is also the 25th percentile.

Quartile (upper) The value of a set of data at the third quarter, 75%, when that data has been arranged in ascending order. It is the median value of the upper half of all the values in the data set. In the lower quartile example, the upper quartile is 19.5, the median value of the upper half of the data set. Three quarters of the marks lie below it. The upper quartile is also the 75th percentile.

Range The difference between the lowest and the highest values in a set of data. For example, for the set of data 12, 15, 23, 30, 31 and 45, the range is the difference between 12 and 45. 12 is subtracted from 45 to give a range of 33.

Ratio A comparison between two numbers or quantities. A ratio is usually expressed in whole numbers. For example, a class consists of 12 boys and 14 girls. The ratio of boys to girls is 12:14. This ratio may be described more simply as 6:7 by dividing both numbers by 2. The ratio of girls to boys is 14:12 or 7:6.

Rounding Expressing a number to a degree of accuracy. This is often done in contexts where absolute accuracy is not required, or not possible. For example, it may be acceptable in a report to give outcomes to the nearest hundred or ten. So the number 674 could be rounded up to 700 to the nearest hundred, or down to 670 to the nearest ten. If a number is half way or more between rounding points, it is conventional to round it up, e.g. 55 is rounded up to 60 to the nearest ten and 3.7 is rounded up to 4 to the nearest whole number. If the number is less than half way, it is conventional to round down, e.g. 16.43 is rounded down to 16.4 to one decimal place.

Scatter graph A graph on which data relating to two variables is plotted as points, each axis representing one of the variables. The resulting pattern of points indicates how the two variables are related to each other. This type of graph is often used to demonstrate or confirm the presence or absence of a correlation between the two variables, and to judge the strength of that correlation.

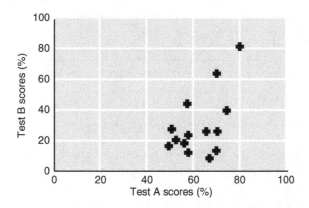

Sector The part or area of a circle which is formed between two radii and the circumference. Each piece of a pie chart is a sector.

Standardised scores Standardised scores are used to enable comparisons on tests between different groups of pupils. Tests are standardised so that the average national standardised scores automatically appear as 100, so it is easy to see whether a pupil is above or below the national average.

Trend The tendency of data to follow a pattern or direction. For example, the trend of the sequence of numbers 4, 7, 11, 13 and 16 is described as 'increasing'.

Value added The relationship between a pupil's previous attainment and their current attainment gives a measure of their progress. Comparing this with the progress made by other pupils gives an impression of the value added by a school. Below is a scatter graph showing progress made by a group of pupils between the end of Key Stage 1 and the end of Key Stage 2:

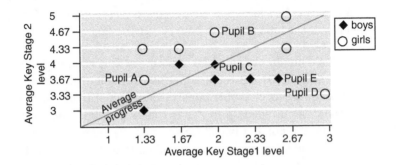

The 'trend line' shows the average performance. Pupils above the line, such as A and B, made better progress than expected; those below the line, such as pupils E and D, made less progress than expected.

How Key Stage 2 relates to Key Stage 1:

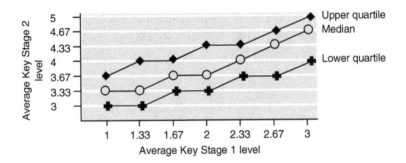

Here the median line shows the national average progress.

Variables The name given to a quantity which can take any one of a given set of values. For example, on a line graph showing distance against time, both distance and time are variables. A variable can also be a symbol which stands for an unknown number, and that can take on different values. For example, the final mark in a test is obtained by a formula using the variables A and B as follows: final mark= (Topic 1 mark x A) + (Topic 2 mark x B).

Weighting A means of attributing relative importance to one or more of a set of results. Each item of data is multiplied by a pre-determined amount to give extra weight to one or more components. For example, marks gained in year 3 of a course may be weighted twice as heavily as those gained in the first two years, in which case those marks would be multiplied by two before finding the total mark for the course.

Whole number A positive integer, e.g. 1, 2, 3, 4, 5.

© Teaching Agency